A Bed By The Sea

A History of Bournemouth's Hotels

Jackie Edwards

NATULA PUBLICATIONS

This edition published in 2010 by Natula Publications, Christchurch, Dorset BH23 1JD

© Jackie Edwards

The right of Jackie Edwards to be identified as the author of this work has been asserted by her in accordance with the Copyright, Designs and Patent Act 1988.

ISBN 9781897887806

A CIP catalogue record of this book is available from the British Library.

Printed by Cpod, Trowbridge, Wiltshire.

Illustrations are from the author's and publisher's collections or with kind permission from The Bournemouth Tourism Department.

Front Cover picture: The West Cliff and Sands, Bournemouth, 1969
Back Cover: Bournemouth Postcard 1910s

Contents

About the Author

Jackie Edwards moved to Bournemouth from Bath in 1993 with her family to run a beautiful Victorian hotel on the East Cliff. She is an active committee member of the local Hotel Association and the East Cliff Residents Association.

A few years ago she moved into an old coach house where she runs a small B&B.

The Coach House Cottage, Bournemouth

Acknowledgements

This book started as a conversation with Councillor Anne Filer where I had asked why no one had written about the hotels in Bournemouth. Straight to the point as usual she said, "Why don't you do it?" So I did!

I would like to thank the following people for their help and support

Jan Marsh
Ken Male
John Walker
Mark Buxton
Hannah Richman
Jane Martin
Michael Green
Members of Bournemouth Area Hospitality Association

Thanks also go to my family, friends and the Bournemouth Tourism Department for all their help. I hope you enjoy reading all about the hotels as much as I enjoyed writing it.

Jackie Edwards
March 2010

Resorts

Seaside resorts in England were born out of a trend and Bournemouth was no exception. 18th century English society had been quick to adopt the idea of the health-giving qualities of sea bathing. Spas such as at Bath had been popular for a long time and entrepreneurs combined the health aspect with a romantic notion of the seaside. The Napoleonic Wars (1799-1815) had meant the wealthy could not travel abroad as easily and so found destinations closer to home. Thus Torquay with its mild winter climate attracted visitors recovering from their illnesses. The Royal Patronage by the Prince of Wales visiting Brighton in 1783 ensured its popularity and by the early 19th century it was one of the fastest growing towns in Britain. In 1848 Brighton was said to have had 250,000 visitors.

Bournemouth Sands 1910

It wasn't however until the 1840s onwards when the railways gave cheap easy access that the resorts really started to expand. Blackpool grew from a small hamlet into a substantial holiday town for the working classes in the industrial north.

1

With the rapid growth of these new seaside resorts, came the expansion in hotels. Hotels, originally from the French word hostel, only started to be recognised in England during the Napoleonic Wars where they provided accommodation for officers on leave and were often run by French refugees. Before this time inns had been the main providers of accommodation. From Roman times inns were used by officials and were found along roads and in main towns. After the Romans left Britain in the 5th century, few people travelled apart from pilgrims who often stayed in abbeys. In the 16th and 17th centuries coaching inns were found on key roads and crossroads with the occasional remote inn for drovers. By the 19th century, hotels providing food, drink and accommodation were sprouting up especially close to the ever-increasing railway stations. With the Victorians and the growth of Industrial Britain the hotels started to reflect society and its aspirations, the higher the social status, the better the hotel, with the wealthy opting for more lavish décor and service.

Bournemouth grew at a phenomenal rate from barren heathland in 1810 to a fashionable health spa then a busy family holiday destination and premier resort. For many years the following quote from the *1968 The Bournemouth Guide* was very true. "The object of the annual holiday is to break the monotony of the normal routine, to get away from places of work, in the cities and towns and to relax. To achieve this a seaside holiday is the most popular, offering a completely different environment to industrialised areas." There may not be so many industrialised areas in Britain now but Bournemouth is still a favourite with all ages as a place to take a holiday break.

Early Days

The Bournemouth of today with its cosmopolitan, vibrant centre and hotels competing fiercely for visitors is in stark contrast to 200 years ago. Then the Bourne Valley was a desolate wilderness of gorse and heath between the old established Boroughs of Christchurch in the east and Poole in the west.

Bournemouth was however, mentioned back in June 1574 in state papers. *"First, we fynde at Bournemouth within the west bay at Christchurch a place very easy for the ennemye to lande there conteyning by estimacion over quarter of myle in length, being voyde of all inhabiting."*

It remained largely uninhabited for a number of years until the 1802 Christchurch Enclosure Act allowed thousands of acres of land to be sold into private ownership for the first time. The 'Liberty of Westover' was mainly agricultural land along the River Stour and heath land. Much of this poor soil had been planted with Scots Pine intended for commercial use. In Bournemouth, William Dean of Littledown House paid £639 for 500 acres including the West Cliff and Sir George Ivison Tapps (Lord of the Manor of Christchurch) paid £1,050 for 205 acres including the East Cliff and Central Bournemouth. Part of the responsibility of landowners was the provision of roads. Roads in the area were very sparse but Poole Lane (Iford to Pokesdown Hill) was to be extended westwards and became the Christchurch to Poole Road. Holdenhurst Road, Bath Road and Richmond Hill along with other roads that became part of modern Bournemouth were created in the years after the Enclosure Act.

In July 1810, retired Army Captain Lewis Tregonwell and his wife (still grief stricken over the death of their baby son Grosvenor) visited the area and were so impressed especially by the little Bourne stream trickling down through the heather to the sea that they decided to buy several acres. The Tregonwells paid Sir George Tapps £179 11s 0d for 8½ acres and thought it ideal for the new fashion of sea bathing. As befitted their wealth they built a summer villa (The Mansion) on the west bank of the Bourne stream and moved into it in April 1812. (It now forms part of the Royal Exeter Hotel.) In 1815 they bought a further picturesque 14 acres and another 13 acres in 1822.

The Tregonwells had Symes Cottage built for their butler. It was later enlarged and became known as Portman Lodge and used by the family and for letting. It was badly damaged by a fire in 1922 and demolished in 1930. The site on the corner of Exeter and Exeter Park Road was used for the bus station, which burnt down in July 1976. It is now a NCP car park in Exeter Road and a proposed site for a new cinema complex.

Terrace Cottage was built for Tregonwell's gardener and then for family members in what is now Upper Terrace Road. The cottage later became part of the much larger Merville Hotel from the 1920s.

Merville Hotel, 1969

In 1939, Hotel Merville boasted 75 bedrooms all with hot and cold running water, gas or electric fires. The dining room seated 200 and there were recreation rooms for dances, billiards and table tennis. The car park was free for up to 30 cars for "those who care to leave their cars in the open" but it cost 1/- per night for the use of a garage. The hotel became badly run down in the late 1970s before being pulled down in 1992 along with its neighbour the Bristol Hotel (formerly Edmondsham House in 1907 then renamed Mayfair Hotel in 1922 and Bristol Hotel from 1961). It is now the site of a car park and part of the Terrace Mount scheme.

Tregonwell found himself accommodating many friends who were delighted with the valley's beauty and the sheltered pine tree walk down to the beach. In 1820 he let his house to the Marchioness of Exeter after whom the house and road are named. It had three parlours, six bedrooms, kitchen, scullery, a stable for two horses, its own cows and a bathing machine. From 1816-1822 Tregonwell built a number of cottages to let to visitors and advertised them in the *Salisbury and Wiltshire Journal*. The early beginnings of Bournemouth's holiday industry had begun.

For the next 25 years the Tregonwell estate was the only real development of the town and covered present day Exeter Road and the land round it bounded by Richmond Hill, Old Christchurch Road and Yelverton Road. It extended up to Commercial Road and south to where the BIC is now.

It wasn't until Sir George William Tapps Gervis (MP for Christchurch) inherited his father's estate in 1835 that the town that we know today started to be developed. Sir George wanted to expand the estate into a seaside health resort similar to Weymouth and Brighton. He employed a young Christchurch architect Benjamin Ferrey. The planning of Bournemouth was Ferrey's first major commission and sites were selected for two hotels and several villas. It was to be a garden city by the sea from the beginning!

Meyrick Road, 1900s

The two men had decided that each villa would be individual and stand in its own grounds. It was due to their careful planning that the beauty of the area was not totally destroyed and that we can still benefit from the woodlands and pines. (Sir George Tapps had planted pine trees in the early part of the 19th century, William Dean doing likewise, as these trees were a commercial crop used as pit props.) Plots of land were sold on long-term ground leases and houses were available to rent by the month for around 4 guineas per week. They were fully furnished but visitors were told to bring their own servants.

The first hotels The Bath Hotel and the Belle Vue Boarding House both opened in 1838. Samuel Bayly built the Belle Vue and he was granted a lease for 80 years. In 1850 it was known as The Belle Vue and Pier Hotel but by 1857 a bankrupt Bayly auctioned it with other properties at The Kings Arms, Christchurch where NS Newlyn bought it. The Bournemouth Corporation

5

purchased it in 1875 to help facilitate their plans for a pavilion by the seafront. In 1924 the top was removed before being completely demolished in 1928 to make way for the Pavilion, which opened in 1929.

The Belle Vue Hotel

The Bath Hotel (built by David Tuck) later became the much bigger Royal Bath Hotel and is still a hotel today. Russell Cotes had an extension built and it was opened on 11th August 1880 by the Lord Mayor of London, who had actually come to Bournemouth to open the Pier. The hotel, at the same time, also changed its name to The Royal Bath and East Cliff Hotel, claiming this was allowed since the Prince of Wales had stayed there in 1856.

The Prince of Wales visiting The Royal Bath Hotel, 1890

The Prince of Wales visited the town on a number of occasions and he had a house built (The Red House) for his mistress Emilie Le Breton Langtry (Lillie Langtry). The romantic hideaway amongst the pine trees in Derby Road, East Cliff is now the Lillie Langtry Hotel. Previously it had been called Manor Heath having been converted into a boarding house in 1938. In 1962 it offered "Edwardian grace with modern comfort" along with "weekly film shows".

The Manor Heath Hotel
(Now The Langtry Manor Hotel)

In 1977 after retiring from flying and teaching pilots Mrs Hamilton Howard changed the hotel's name and refurbished it in the style Edward and Lillie would have recognised. Many original features were kept including the extra wide doors to accommodate the large dresses of the day. The Kings Room was restored to its original size and the huge inglenook fireplace was once again on display. For the 21st century the boutique hotel has however updated the rooms with a contemporary twist notably in the bathrooms.

The Royal Bath Hotel, meanwhile, was a place where Russell Cotes enjoyed showing off his art collection to the wealthy and elite visitors, having purchased the hotel on Christmas Day 1876. Inside the hotel it was beautifully painted with murals, the dining room a replica of the Egyptian Hall at the London Mansion House and a large area of the ground floor was devoted to a Japanese collection that in 1891 was worth £300,000. As many rooms as possible were to have sea views so long corridors were necessary but were all decorated with pictures and other works of art.

The Royal Bath Hotel, 1910

The King's Hall

Famous visitors included Empress Eugenie of France (wife of Napoleon III of France), King and Queen of Sweden, the Duke and Duchess of Westminster (richest family in Victorian England), Gladstone, Sir Henry

Irving, a famous actor and theatre manager, and Oscar Wilde. Wilde wrote of the Royal Bath Hotel in 1878, "You have built and fitted up with the greatest beauty and elegance, a palace and filled it with gems of art for the use and benefit of the public." Wilde also stayed at The Newlyns Family Hotel in 1883.

The Royal Bath Hotel, 1920

In 1906 it had a hotel orchestra that played every evening, an up-to-date electric lift and abolished the charge for lights. However by the 1960s Russell Cotes' granddaughter Mrs Lee Duncan was finding it a strain maintaining the five-star hotel and it was in danger of being downgraded by the AA. In 1962 her plans to turn it into a block of flats were turned down and in 1963 she sold the hotel to the De Vere Group. They spent £200,000 bringing it back up to five-star status, adding a casino in the King's Hall. The new manager in 1969, Mr Lloyd Jones, realised that the conference trade was where the hotel needed to concentrate and to achieve this he had the casino moved upstairs to the former housekeepers rooms, where it remained until it closed in the 1990s. On 20th January 1979 a huge fire destroyed around ⅓ of the hotel. 18 guests and 40 staff were led to safety. A million pounds later the hotel was ready to be re-opened in April 1980. The Royal Bath continued with improvements and in 1988 a new leisure complex was completed in the gardens. The hotel was advertising butler service in seven luxury suites in December 1997. It did eventually lose one of its stars but it is still a grand building.

In 1841 an important physician called Dr Augustus Bozzi Granville was writing a book on spas of England. He was invited to stay in the "almost unknown sea watering place". He included Bournemouth in his second volume as a perfect place for people with chest problems. The pine trees with their balmy, resinous odour were seen as extremely beneficial to those with bronchial problems (a condition very common in the 19th century). The climate was also very mild in winter and the breezes in summer kept the temperatures to a moderate level. He also wrote, "Water of the brook is from the gravel and sandy beds below the peat on adjoining heath, on which not a particle of manure is ever spread."

The 1840s saw a surge in affluent visitors and invalids seeking out the healthy sea and pine-scented air. Fields were drained south of what is now the Square to form walks and shrubberies and a bridge built in 1849 over the Bourne stream. The first guide (*Sydenhams*) was published in 1840.

Lord Meyrick's home at Hinton Admiral

However even by the 1850s there were only 3 hotels in Bournemouth, The Bath known as The Hotel, The Belle Vue known as The Boarding House and the London Hotel known as the London and Commercial Inn. The London Hotel was on the junction of Commercial and Avenue Road. It had been enlarged in 1875 and by 1926 was known as the London Hotel, Grill and Restaurant, before being demolished in 1930. The son of a former owner recollected driving four horse carriages from the hotel to its stables in Avenue Road. The site was rebuilt and housed John Collier's men's shop, then Burtons and is now a Vodaphone outlet.

The population of Bournemouth in 1851 was only 695 and they were adamant they did not want a railway. The Commissioners believed that by encouraging Sunday Excursions it: "would necessitate opening of public houses and refreshment rooms and interfere with quietness of Sabbath, not at all conductive to the best interests of the town." The railway from Southampton to Dorchester served Ringwood, Wimborne and Wareham with a branch line to Hamworthy which connected with Poole via a ferry and toll bridge. Passengers had to either endure a 12 mile coach journey from the nearest station (Holmsley, now tearooms) to The Bath Hotel or use the Hamworthy branch line. In 1870 a small station was built near the brickworks on the Holdenhurst Road and served as a terminus from Ringwood. It wasn't until 1888 that Bournemouth received a direct railway line from Southampton via Brockenhurst linking Bournemouth East (a new station building opened 1885 but known from 1899 as Bournemouth Central) and Bournemouth West (opened 1874) stations. The railway line remained discreet. The plans for a central station near Braidley Road were never carried out.

Merton Russell Cotes, the owner of the Bath Hotel, had encouraged the direct line and persuaded Sir George Meyrick to allow LSWR to cross his estates with the promise of a station near his home at Hinton Admiral. Russell Cotes knew there was money to be made for his hotel from visitors using the railway. By 1856 it was deemed that the town should move away from its invalid's image and promote more of the summer season which was poor compared to the winter. The Bournemouth Improvement Act 1856 allowed 13 commissioners control "within the circle of the radius of a mile, whereof the centre is the front door of the Belle Vue Hotel." They appointed Christopher Creeke as Surveyor and Inspector of Nuisances. He was an expert on roads and drains and given the responsibility of planning new roads in the developing town. Impressed with Creeke's energy William Dean appointed him special advisor to the Dean Estate.

Bournemouth was, however, even by 1860 a quiet town with no meeting places or even a promenade. Although Creeke supported an Undercliff Drive from Alum Chine to Boscombe, William Dean and John Tregonwell opposed it as unnecessary and a waste of ratepayers' money. By 1882 an engineer Mr Birch who had designed the newly built pier put forward a scheme funded

privately. It would have a museum, aquarium, bathing place and buildings for
the arts, sciences and healthy pursuits paid for by an entrance fee. The
Commissioners asked Dean for permission to build on the sea front at the
West Cliff with a public footpath at St Michael's Road and Durley Chine Road.
But even in 1887 Dean was still against building the Undercliff Road,
preferring money to be spent on the crumbling cliff. Agreement wasn't
reached until 1901 with Dean's successor James Edward Cooper Dean. In
1907 the road was opened between Meyrick Road and Bournemouth Pier and
from there to the boundary with the Cooper Dean West Cliff estate in 1911.

East Cliff Zig Zag path, 1910

Other sections of the Promenade followed and in 1919 Cooper Dean
eventually granted permission for it to continue from the Pier to Alum Chine.
Ellen Cooper Dean formally opened it in 1930. Other pieces of land were
leased to the Council at a reduced rent providing they were kept as open public
spaces and they included the junction of Durley and West Cliff Road, the West
Cliff frontage from Durley Chine to the Highcliff Hotel and a triangular piece
of land from Commercial Road's junction with Durley Road.

Bournemouth's Hotel History

Central Bournemouth

With the expansion of Bournemouth as a favoured resort amongst the affluent Victorian society a new magnificent hotel was planned and in 1881 Oscar II King of Sweden laid the foundation stone for the Mont Dore Hotel. It was designed in the Italian style by the architect Alfred Bedborough and built by London and Bristol builders Messrs Howell and Sons. The "hotel in the glen" was to have every conceivable luxury including one of the first telephones (its number was 3). The hotel's name came from the Mont Dore Cure (a treatment from the volcano region of the Auvergne France) that it offered. When the hotel was put up for public auction in June 1886 the extensive baths were in a separate building and included Turkish baths, "the best in England", medicated seawater (despite being 500 yards from the sea there was a direct connection), plunge baths and others. The Mont Dore Cure would be beneficial to those with consumption, rheumatism, gout and bronchial problems.

Mont Dore Hotel
Now Bournemouth Town Hall

13

The sale on behalf of the mortgagees was offered to capitalists, hotel proprietors and others as a sound and lucrative investment. The hotel had attracted a large number of: "the best class of visitor". The "tripping season" was seen as August to September with the superior class being the winter residents who would have left by Easter. They were no doubt pampered in the 120 beds and sitting rooms many of which overlooked the sea. The hotel boasted a ballroom, billiards, reading room, four tennis courts including a covered court, bowling green and outdoor skating. This was all set in four acres of mature pine trees overlooking the public gardens. One of its regular guests was Marie Lloyd who reputedly told the man sent every week to wind the hotel's thirty six clocks that he couldn't come into her room whilst she was dressing!

ROYAL NATIONAL SANATORIUM, BOURNEMOUTH. (MAIN ENTRANCE)

Royal National Sanatorium

In 1904 The General Manger of Mont Dore complained about the appearance and general coughing of inmates at the adjoining National Sanatorium as being offensive to his guests. This first ever purpose built sanatorium opened in 1855 for the treatment of consumption and diseases of the chest. Legal action was threatened and blinds placed across windows in the Sanatorium. Bournemouth was in the process of changing its image as a resort just for invalids.

Mont Dore was requisitioned during the First World War on 20th November 1914 as a hospital for Indian forces. After the Indian Army Corps withdrew from France in 1915, it became a British Military Hospital and in 1918 a convalescent home for British officers. From November 1918 until it closed in May 1919 many of the patients were officers repatriated from POW camps. The wounded were brought to Mont Dore from the railway station either by one of the few motor ambulances or by a charabanc and were carried up the steeply curved staircases, as the lift was often out of order.

One patient was William Joseph Punch an aborigine who fought for Australia in the war. He had been the sole survivor of a brutal attack on his family in 1880 and had been brought up by a white family in New South Wales. He was described as a respected worker, sportsman and accomplished musician before signing up on 31st December 1915. Wounded twice, first in Belgium then on 5th April in France he was brought to England to be treated. He however died of pneumonia on 29th August 1917 aged 37 in Mont Dore Hospital and was buried in Plot X, grave number 185, amongst other Commonwealth graves in Bournemouth East Cemetery.

The Mont Dore never opened as a hotel again; it was sold in 1921 for £33,000 to Bournemouth Corporation and become the Town Hall.

Central Gardens

Bournemouth for a number of years attracted visitors including many well-known people, predominantly to improve their health. Aubrey Beardsley the artist stayed in July 1876 at Pier View Hotel overlooking Boscombe Pier where he worked by candlelight. He was 24 years old and seriously ill with TB. He wasn't impressed with the area though, writing, "I am beginning to feel that I shall be an exile from all nice places for the rest of my days. Boscombe is only tolerable, I am so disappointed with it."

Pier Hotel, 1960

In January 1897 he was moved to a guesthouse Muriel (Cheam House) just off Bournemouth Square. Rebbeck had built it in the 1860s for the Tregonwell's estate bailiff. It had a quirky feature of having 3 front doors all on different levels. In the 1890s it was furnished apartments before undergoing various uses such as an accountant's office, theatrical bookings office, and home to a model railway and gift shop. The plans to turn it into a pub in 1975 were rejected and it was demolished in 1995. There is a now plaque on the site at the junction of Exeter Road and Terrace Road.

In 1884 RL Stevenson, who never enjoyed the best of health, stayed at the Iffley boarding house on West Cliff Road before moving to The Firs in West Cliff Gardens. He later lived at Skerryvore in Westbourne. A bomb destroyed it in 1940, but a plaque can be found in the public gardens there. Stevenson wrote *A Child's Garden of Verse*, *Kidnapped* and *The Strange Case of Dr. Jekyll and Mr Hyde* whilst in Bournemouth.

The poet Rupert Brooke visited his Uncle Richard England Brooke and Aunt Fanny at Grantchester Dene, 12 Littledown Road from 1895-1914. He is best known for his famous poems about The Old Vicarage at Grantchester and *The Soldier*.

> If I should die, think only this of me:
> That there's some corner of a foreign field
> That is forever England.
>
> (from *The Soldier*)

In 1906 Brooke wrote describing Bournemouth as, "a strange place which is full of moaning pines, and impressionist but quite gentlemanly sunsets. With other decrepit and grey haired invalids I drift wanly along the cliffs." His relatives' house later became holiday flats and is now 48 Dean Park Road.

Grantchester Dene

With the town's popularity, its choice of accommodation and attractions were found in various guidebooks. The *1886 Heywoods Guide to Bournemouth* advertised the town as: "The wants of humbler visitors are catered for, though not to so great an extent as in the older seaside towns." The average stay would cost 2½ guineas per week. In 1888, *Brights Illustrated Guide to Bournemouth* wrote that the greater number of larger houses to let were on the East Cliff with six winter month lets from 5-25 guineas per week. The largest numbers of Boarding Houses (residential premises with both shelter and food provided) were on the West Cliff. There were also houses let whole or in apartments (holiday homes that were usually serviced) from 4-17 guineas per room per week. Messrs Atkey and Roker of Bank Chambers (near the Square) periodically issued fresh registers of furnished and unfurnished houses to be let or sold.

By 1888 Bournemouth was showing signs of its phenomenal growth as a resort with *Brights* pointing out: "Hardly an evening passes without a concert or lecture in New Town Hall (the old Theatre Royal in Albert Road with room for 1,600 people), Shaftesbury Hall and Gymnasium (in Gervis Road and capable of holding 1,000 people) or one of the many parochial or school rooms." There was a bicycle and tricycle club, chess club, political clubs with billiard and reading rooms. "Choral, scientific and mutual improvement societies hold evening meetings during the greater part of the year."

Schools were also on the increase with Bournemouth High School for Boys in Westbourne Road where to: "guard as far as possible against infectious or contagious disease, a certificate being required from every boy before he enters the school each term." Poyntington in West Hill Road was an "Anglo Indian Home and School for the sons of gentlemen." The avant-garde French poet Paul Verlaine came to Bournemouth in 1876 after his release from

Cadogan Hotel, 1969

prison for shooting his friend Arthur Rimbaud in the wrist for threatening to leave him. He taught French at Reverend Remington's private school St Aloysius, No. 2 Westbourne Terrace. Later it became the Sandbourne Hotel and then renamed the Cadogan Hotel until it was demolished (along with the East Anglia Hotel) and a Premier Inn built in its place in 2008.

In the *1890 Mates Bournemouth Illustrated* there were listed 32 comfortable guesthouses

The East Anglia Hotel, 1930

listed, nine of which were hotels. 21 being run by women, as this was a way they could maintain their own financial independence. It is interesting to note that whilst the women were in the Burgess Rolls they did not have the vote.

In the *1890 Sydenham Guide* it was remarked that, "The proprietors seem to vie with each other in their endeavour to provide for the comfort of their patrons!" Weekly terms including meals went from £2 11s 6d to £3 12s 6d for a single room and £5 5s 0d to £7 7s 0d for a double room.

In 1890 the 'Chinese Giant' moved to Bournemouth for health reasons. Chang Woo Gow was 8 foot tall and weighed 26 stone. He toured the world for 25 years before moving to Moyuen (now Ashleigh Hotel) in Southcote Road. He lived there for three years and opened a Chinese tearoom. After the death of his wife, he died a few months later from a broken heart, aged 53, and is buried in Bournemouth Cemetery.

Ashleigh Hotel, 1968

Chang's tearooms were amongst many diverse trades in Bournemouth at the time. Visitors and residents could use: R Tyrell & Sons "Dress, Warehousemen & General Drapers" in Old Christchurch Road; Mr C Knowlman a hatter, hosier, glover, shirtmaker and athletic outfitter at 79 Old Christchurch Road; RH White a brewer, wine and spirit merchant at Bournemouth Brewery, Holdenhurst Road; Mr P Beti "Au Chalet Suisse, Patissier and Confiseur" at 5 & 6 The Arcade and Mr W Townsend "Oyster Merchant at The Oyster Plume, The Square" where you could also book pleasure coach trips.

Old Christchurch Road, 1908

Mr Albert Green at Verulam House, Yelverton Road was a taxidermist and dealer in British and foreign birds and goldfish. The Trinity Restaurant at 141 Old Christchurch Road served "fish dinners as low as 6d and very delicious." They also offered "sleeping arrangements" with "every care is taken to ensure that the beds are thoroughly comfortable and well aired".

Bournemouth Square, 1913

In 1883 Marguerite Radclyffe Hall the novelist was born at Sunny Lawn House, now Durley Grange Hotel, Durley Road. Her most famous book was *The Well of Loneliness*. Based on her own life, it is still a well-known book on lesbianism. By 1896 the house was called Durley Grange and was a boarding house run by Miss Ivatt and Miss Beales, it was advertised as being situated in pleasant own grounds with good drawing, dining and smoking rooms. Special arrangements could be made for long-term stays.

Sunny Lawn

In January 1898 Marconi established a station at Madeira House near the pier, (now Court Royal convalescent home). At the same time Gladstone was staying in Bournemouth but was seriously ill. Snowstorms destroyed the telegraph wires between Bournemouth and London and Marconi sent the journalists' reports on Gladstone's terminal illness to the Needles Wireless Telegraph Station, making Marconi responsible for the first ever radio news. Later Marconi had disagreements with the management and moved the station to a nearby house called Sandhills, which was later demolished to make way for the BIC.

In the 1890s hotels offered accommodation with hot and cold running water, hydropathic baths and some electric light, public rooms and a sanitary inspection certificate. Priory Mansions Boarding Establishment on the corner of Bath Road, St. Peter's Road and Gervis Road advertised in *Bright's Guide to*

Bournemouth 1888 as: "Drainage carried out upon best sanitary principles, the house holds a certificate for sanitary excellence."

Court Royal, 1900s

Priory Mansions, 1930

Bournemouth had a fair number of Temperance Hotels. In 1896 in the *Bournemouth Illustrated*, The Granville on Richmond Hill (now offices) proudly advertised itself as: "Best appointed Temperance Hotel in the Kingdom."

Meanwhile the Midland Temperance Hotel was: "fitted up with every modern requirement, corridors heated with hot water and all the principal rooms are lighted with electricity. Drawing, reading, coffee, commercial and billiard rooms. Omnibuses pass near hotel to all parts of town every ten minutes through the day."

Visitors were warned in *Mates Hampshire & Isle of Wight Illustrated 1899* that rowing boats could be hired from the shore or landing stage at the pier. It being "more sensible to adopt latter course for if the sea is at all rough, and it very often is, one is liable to get a wet jacket at starting, while landing is rather worse, the boats having a tendency to going ashore broadside on, instead of bow first, the result being sometimes disastrous in the case of inexperienced hands. A good deal of fishing is done from the end of the pier by juveniles and large numbers of smelt and whiting are taken. Hire a boat and go to Whiting Rocks."

The Sands and East Cliff, Bournemouth.

Bournemouth Sands, 1900s

The *1906 Bournemouth Guide* was still extolling the health benefits of the town: "To delicate children and to those enfeebled by the worries of life, and especially to those suffering from insomnia, Bournemouth maybe a perfect haven of restoration and cure." In the *Daily Mail* on 25th July 1906 a letter was published: "In the drawing room of my hotel lies an elegantly bound devotional book, with this inscription 'to the visitors at ... Hotel, from one of themselves in gratitude to God for restored health when hope was long over past.'"

In 1911 the local directory listed 80 hotels and 256 guesthouses, boarding houses and apartments. The Washington Hotel in Durley Road advertised their rates as one and a half guineas per week with an Angelus piano player and a splendid selection of records. Mr & Mrs Meggitt offered special terms for winter visitors. There were separate tables and smoking rooms.

The following year the guide was writing, "No town is better kept, the cleanliness of the streets is a delight to the eye. How Bournemouth runs thousands of acres of pleasure grounds, three golf links, two piers, municipal bands with a salary list of £7,000 a year and almost noiseless electric trams on a five shilling rate is a pleasing municipal mystery."

Central Gardens, 1911

In January 1912, the writer DH Lawrence came to Bournemouth for a month to convalesce. He had been suffering from double pneumonia and had been gravely ill. He wrote several letters to his friend Louie Burrows describing his daily routine at his hotel, Compton House, St Peter's Road. Lawrence describes other residents at the hotel and the custom of taking tea in one of the town's many restaurants. By 17th January he wrote that he had been moved into a larger room and his rash had got better! (In all his letters he writes of his improving health.) He is also very happy with the hotel as it gives him "real privacy". By 20th January he sends a postcard of Christchurch (where he had recently spent the day) describing his trip to Poole Harbour. He also changes his views on Bournemouth from being like a huge hospital with invalids at every corner to being a jolly and pretty town.

Invalids Walk, 1916

Compton House, 1915

Whilst in Bournemouth he wrote 300 pages of his book, *The Trespasser*. The hotel was demolished and in 1973 the eight storey circular office block Compton House was built (Now Mercury House).

Even in the 1922-23 *Ward Lock Guide* Bournemouth was still extolling its virtues as a health resort and being "ozone aired" and having reasonable rents, a punctual railway service and "the almost fastidious hygiene". Crag Hall advertised electric light, separate tables, good baths and strictly moderate terms for either a comfortable holiday or permanent home. There are a few hotels in this early guide still trading with their original name such as Silver How, West Cliff Gardens, "delightful situation, well sheltered" and from £2 2s 0d per week including electric lights. During the years when Mr James Kirkwood Hume was resident its name was Silverhew. During the Second World War it is reputed that Clark Gable was billeted here. He had been sent to England to make a film on aerial gunners in 1943.

Silver How, 1906

However it is also said that Clark Gable stayed at The Palace Court Hotel where he was severely reprimanded by the head housekeeper checking that the blackouts were all in place and caught the actor smoking on the balcony!

The Woodcroft in Gervis Road had grounds of about 2 acres with tennis and croquet lawns. They had an "excellent cuisine and liberal table." Telegrams were listed as "Safety Bournemouth" or phone 202. The hotel is still there but with some of its gardens now used for parking.

The Belvedere on Bath Road was advertising a "High class establishment charmingly situated amongst the pines. Special attention is given to the cuisine and the culinary arrangements are of the most modern and up to date. The house is heated during winter by hot water radiators and electric light in every room." (It had previously been a private house in 1857 lived in by a Mrs Lumsden, in 1890 it was home to Caroline Moseley but by 1903 Mr Heath advertised it as apartments to rent. Mrs Lincoln was running it as boarding establishment by 1905.) In the *Bournemouth Guide 1912* it was owned by Mrs Millership where it was situated in its own grounds in the sheltered East Cliff and charged 2-3½ guineas per week. By 1924 Mr and Mrs Drawbridge advertised: "freedom and comfort of guest guaranteed." By 1929 Mr and Mrs Barratt offered free baths.

Belvedere Hotel

The Collingwood Private Hotel was in Kerley Road in 1922 and advertised the property as overlooking the sea and pier. It was also one of the many boarding houses still being run by women. In 1894 it had been owned for a number of years by Emma Farnell and called Glenmore. By the 1950s it had become a nursing home and is now offices.

The name however was transferred to a new hotel in Priory Road, formed by joining the houses Blenheim (formerly Audley which had been home to Mr Henry John Fowler in 1891) and Thornham to Peel Court in the 1950s, becoming The Collingwood Hotel.

The Collingwood Private Hotel in Kerley Road, 1930

The Collingwood Hotel in Priory Road, 1968

West Cliff

Having lived in the town since 1832, Mr Christopher Crabbe Creeke, as official surveyor, was determined not to ruin Bournemouth's best features. He studied Granville's suggestion and had the central pleasure gardens laid out. He then also helped undertake the development of William Dean's West Cliff estate.

The Pine Walk, West Cliff, Bournemouth.

Pine Walk, West Cliff, 1900s

Creeke disliked straight roads, preferring tree lined avenues, crescents and circular gardens (Cavendish Road and Horseshoe Common). He planned a new road, Durley Chine Road running up from the coast to Poole Road and along to what is now the Wessex Way. Creeke envisaged West Cliff Road having back-to-back residential crescents, wide tree lined roads and public gardens. As a planner his schemes were lavish and used an excessive amount of valuable land.

In 1891 the three members of the Homray family living at Winterdyne had three resident servants. It became a hotel in 1935 and run by Mr and Mrs Le Tourneaux in 1945.

Although William Dean did not accept all of Creek's grandiose ideas he took his advice on the creation of 99-year leases instead of selling the freeholds. He had naively made the mistake of selling 137 acres at below market price to Robert Kerley in 1856 and selling four acres (including what is now West Cliff Gardens) in 1860 to Thomas Rawlins. After Rawlins death in 1881 his house West Cliff Cottage was pulled down and a block of terraces surrounded by villas built. Many of these became boarding houses including The Paragon where in 1896 it was advertised as being amongst the "salubrious pines, close to West Cliff bathing machines, sea views in all parts of house which is thoroughly ventilated and suitably heated".

Winter Dene Hotel, 1950s

Paragon, 1927

The Pinehurst in 1908 had thirty bedrooms and a billiard and recreational room and charged from 30/- to 42/- according to the position of the room. The Whitely was a "first class apartment house" run by Mr Gordon for "moderate terms". Tower House had thirty bedrooms in 1911 and a luxurious lounge. Terms were from one and a half guineas and Mr & Mrs Law urged visitors to send telegrams to "Lawful Bournemouth".

By 1862 building plots had been leased in Chine Crescent Road, Durley Road and Chine Road. West Hill Road, Poole Hill and Purbeck Road were also developed with the intention that the local builders leasing the plots would build small houses with shops that were similar in design.

Development was also taking place on Tregonwell land. Peter Tuck in around 1856 built two semi-detached cottages called Cliftonville 3 and 4 (now part of The Hermitage Hotel but previously known as Southcliffe Hall) and two other cottages Cliftonville 1 and 2 which were demolished in 1928 when the White Hermitage Hotel was enlarged and also to make room for a car park. The land where the Hermitage Hotel and Punshon House stand had formerly belonged to the Earl of Malmesbury. Punshon House was built in the 1890s and run for fifteen years by George Harding and son. It was the Vale Royal Hotel before being used for adult education in the 1980s and 1990s and has now been renovated and re-opened as the Park Central Hotel.

Vale Royal Hotel

Brookside (now absorbed by the Hermitage Hotel) was a high-class boarding house in 1866 when John Keble a renowned Theologian and Leader of the Oxford Movement died there. He had sought to return the Anglican Church to High Church ideals and retired in ill health to Bournemouth. In

January 1866 he wrote, "We are not at all repent of having come here. The climate has been unusually moist and mild and we have comforts we would not have at Penzance." In 1896 Brookside was furnished apartments "well sheltered in winter". Many years later for thirty years it had been used for staff accommodation until in 1997 the owner Mr Oram gave it a million pound renovation.

White Hermitage Hotel, 1930

Peter Tuck built and lived for a time in Willow Cottage at the top of what is now Commercial Road. In 1878 Willow Cottage and Willowside formed the site of The Tregonwell Arms Temperance Hotel. It remained a hotel and restaurant until the 1970s but is now the site of the shop Oswald Bailey.

The Victoria Hotel, 1971

In 1864 Mr Tuck purchased Exeter House and its four acres of land on 99-year leases at £130 p.a. from Henrietta Tregonwell and her son John. He separated the land from Exeter House and proceeded to build large villas. The circular access road was divided into nine segments (now Exeter Park Road). The first house was sold in 1866 to William Wheaton a bookseller from Ringwood. He named it Lauderdale but sold it a year later to Mr Druitt of Mayfair and Mr Mayo an official in the India office. In 1894 a John Armytage Crawshaw was living there. It is now The Lampeter Hotel. In the *Bournemouth Guide* for 1915 Miss Seekings, the manageress, advertised it as: "A commodious detached residence situated in its own grounds, commanding position overlooking the beautiful public pleasure gardens. Rooms bright, cheerful and well furnished. 20 visitors beds, dining room separate tables. From 5/6d per day for short periods or a double room 3 guineas per week." On 19th October 1993 a fire swept through the hotel bar but the twenty elderly guests were led to safety.

Lampeter Hotel

Allegria (Whitehall Hotel) was built around the same time as Lauderdale. It overlooked Exeter Park Road and the Pleasure Gardens. Allegria was granted a licence to open as a hotel in 1877 for a Henry Richards. Later in 1891 it was home to a Mr Thomas Evans Bethell. It was possibly the first hotel in this area and was enlarged in 1926, 1929 and 1931. It seems to have changed its name to the Whitehall Hotel sometime after the First World War as previously there had been a White Hall on the East Cliff. It has had many architectural changes over the years demonstrated by its mixture of Italianate and Dutch styles. The hotel undertook major rebuilding in 1938 with the curved gable removed and the roof tower replaced with crenulations. In 1949 it was seen as having expanded enough and it was refused permission to enlarge anymore. In 1924 it had been granted permission to be joined to its neighbouring hotel The Lampeter (both owned by Mr Sydney Brown) but it was never undertaken. In 1926 The Lampeter had new owners, the Popes who extended the hotel with a new wing and sun lounge. Plans for a 3-storey extension on the front in 1938 were shelved. The hotel remained in the same family until the 1960s.

Arlington Hotel

Both the Arlington (still has the same name) and of course Brookside (part of the Hermitage Hotel) were built by Peter Tuck. The Burgess Register has Isabella Mildmay living at Brookside in 1894. (It is said that Thomas Hardy used Brookside as a setting for a murder scene in *Tess of the d'Urbevilles* in 1891.) The Arlington, despite the owners having ambitions for alterations over the years, only had its dining room extended as late as 1973. In the 1920 guide The Arlington at Exeter Park, South Cliff was: "thoroughly well equipped and comfortable, facing due South and West amongst the pines on Main Avenue through the Central Pleasure Gardens. First class cuisine, every comfort at three guineas for a single room and six guineas for a double room."

Two more villas were built fronting Exeter Road: The Hive (a boarding house for a while and then the Bournemouth Local Association Head Quarters for Boy Scouts) and The Waterford. In the 1930s until 1935 The Waterford was a boarding house. The villas were demolished and a new Punshon Church (opened 1958) was built on the site. In 1877 a star shaped house called St Clair was built. It later became a boarding house and was sold in 1937 for £2,000 and renamed the Exeter Grange Hotel. It is now Exeter Grange flats.

Exeter Grange Hotel, 1939

Tregonwell's original house The Mansion had been leased to the Marchioness of Exeter and after she died in 1837 it became a school. In 1871 it was granted a licence for £140 p.a. to become a hotel. Peter Tuck then sold the lease on to Nicholas Newlyn (who owned the King's Arms Hotel in Christchurch) for £1,800 with a 91-year lease at £200 p.a. ground rent. It was renamed Newlyn's Family Hotel. He had the building enlarged and in 1886 Henry Newlyn (his son) had the centre built up into a crenulated tower. Wings were added and the lawn lowered making it a 4-storey building.

In 1888 Henry Newlyn advertised that for seven years he had been caterer to HRH Prince of Wales, HRH Duke of Cambridge, HRH Prince Edward of Saxe Weimar and the officers of her Majesty's Brigade of Guards, Guards Club London in *Brights Illustrated Guide to Bournemouth*. Also that year Henry Newlyn of the Exeter Park Hotel (formerly Newlyn's Family Hotel) asked magistrates to re-register the hotel as "The Royal and Imperial Park Hotel" after Empress Elisabeth of Austria took over the whole building for nine days. Problems arose with the Empress of Austria's attendants who placed pictures on the

NEWLYN'S ROYAL-AND IMPERIAL HOTEL BOURNEMOUTH.

gardener, one of a cow on his front and one of seawater on his back. They poked him on the chest or slapped him on his back to indicate what they wanted. This may have spurred the hotel to employ three interpreters to help foreign visitors.

In 1889 the Newlyns wrote to the Empress offering their condolences on the death (suicide) of her eldest son Archduke Rudolf.

Bournemouth.
Hants

To
Her Majesty
The Empress & Queen of
Austria & Hungary

May I plead that your
Majesty
will accept my humble
but heartfelt sympathy
in this sudden bereavement.
I have only once seen &
served you for a short time
but my whole heart & prayers
go to you now, through this
time of trial & terrible sorrow
Your very humble & devoted servant
Leonie A. Newlyn

Jan 31st 1889.

36

Mrs Newlyn received a letter in reply from the Royal Household:

> Hofburg
> Vienna
> 9' of February
> 1889
>
> Madame!
>
> His Excellency Baron Nopcsa
> instructed me to thank You
> for the kind and warm words
> You have been good enough
> to forward to Her Majesty the
> Empress in connection with
> the lamentable death of the
> Crownprince. Her Majesty
> was visible touched by
> Your verry kind words and
> gave the ordre to express
> Her warmest thanks.

The Empress Elisabeth had given permission for her royal standard to be flown every Sunday at the hotel until her return. However she never did come back as she was stabbed and killed in Geneva in 1898 by an Italian anarchist.

In 1889 the building was refurbished in: "the most artistic and luxurious manner". By 1893 it had been fitted with electric light. In *An Illustrated Account of Bournemouth* (1893) it had "the complete system of telephonic communication which brings its inmates in touch with the establishment of those physicians for whom the district is celebrated". There were eight luxurious private sitting rooms and "no less than forty lofty and well ventilated sleeping apartments, replete with every comfort". There were: "special and inclusive arrangements are made for visitors' servants and children. In connection with the hotel is ample stabling accommodation, the buildings being erected to the most improved hygienic principles, and under the charge of thoroughly experienced ostlers."

The Royal Exeter Hotel

Palm Court, Royal Exeter Hotel, 1925

In the *1895 Stevens Directory* the hotel was advertised as offering "hospitality to the nobility and aristocracy of Europe, England and America". Guests included The Duke of Connaught, Queen Victoria's son, who was in Bournemouth to open a wing of the Royal Victoria Hospital. Maintaining such high standards and more extensions must have proved costly as by the following year the hotel was mortgaged to the Wilts and Dorset bank!

In 1911 the owner William Cox had a glass extension on pillars built on the right hand side of the front. It was taken down in 1923 and a new east wing built.

The 1920s saw the formation of the Exeter Hotel Company and by 1923 the hotel had 74 bedrooms and a new 12-sided Palm Court. The hotel changed its name during the First World War from the Royal and Imperial Exeter Park Hotel to the Royal Exeter Hotel.

In December 1931 a jewel thief armed with a revolver was arrested at the hotel where he had disguised himself as a woman.

The 1935 tariff (below) show that visitors were important in the winter months including terms charged for servants and chauffeurs!

APARTMENTS AND À LA CARTE CHARGES	EN PENSION TERMS
Single Room, including Bath ... ... from **8/6** to **12/6**	Single Room / Double Room } **18/6, 20/-, 21/6, 22/6, 23/6, 24/6 and 25/6** per person.
Double Room, ,, ,, ... ,, **17/-** ,, **25/-**	The above Terms include : Apartments, Bath, Breakfast, Luncheon, Afternoon Tea and Table d'Hôte Dinner, and are not quoted for a stay of less than three full days.
Private Sitting Room, including all Service ... from **22/6**	
Breakfast, Table d'Hôte **4/-**	
Breakfast, Plain, with Preserves **3/-**	
Luncheon, Table d'Hôte **4/-**	**WINTER MONTHS.**
Afternoon Tea **1/-**	October 1st to March 31st, excluding Christmas and Easter, for a stay of not less than One Week.
Dinner, Table d'Hôte **7/6**	Rooms at 18/6 per day are reduced to **£5 15 6** per week
À la carte Meals served at any time.	20/- ,, ,, ,, ,, **£6 10 0** ,, ,,
	21/6 ,, ,, ,, ,, **£7 0 0** ,, ,,
FIRES. Whole Day, 3/- Half Day, 2/- Evening, 1/6.	22/6 ,, ,, ,, ,, **£7 7 0** ,, ,,
	23/6 ,, ,, ,, ,, **£7 17 6** ,, ,,
SERVICE.	24/6 ,, ,, ,, ,, **£8 0 0** ,, ,,
Breakfast served in Bedroom ... ... **6d.** per person	25/6 ,, ,, ,, ,, **£8 10 0** ,, ,,
Luncheon and Dinner served in Bedroom **1/-** ,, ,, ,,	
No Charge is made for Plain Breakfast served in Bedroom.	**SERVANTS.** 14/6 per day inclusive.
	CHAUFFEURS. Room and Board at Garage, 8/6 per day.
HOTEL INFORMATION.	**CHILDREN** under 10 years of age are charged by special arrangement.
Garage for 100 cars close by Hotel, replete with every convenience.	**DOGS** are accommodated but charged for, and are allowed in all the Public Rooms, except the Restaurant, if on leash.
All Rooms are fitted with Hot and Cold Running Water, and Gas Fires or Central Heating.	
Cheques received in Payment of Account by arrangement.	No Allowance can be made from the Pension Terms for any Meals not taken.

Reservations can be made through any Office of Thos. Cook and Sons, Ltd.

Apartment charges, Royal Exeter Hotel, 1935

The hotel was sold to Mr Richard Carr for £55,000 in September 1943 and was extensively modernised and refurbished including turning the Palm Court into a ballroom. In May 1952 the building was listed as Grade II. Permission was sought in 1958 to convert the hotel into 29 self-contained flats and a maisonette. This was agreed in principle and in 1959 plans were granted for 31 self-contained flats. On 7th June 1960 plans for an 18-storey block incorporating a hotel and conference centre were rejected and the appeal on 25th November 1960 failed. However due to ill health Mr Richard Carr retired and Mr and Mrs Leonard Carr who had been at the Meyrick Cliffs Hotel in Beacon Road took over the running of the hotel. The hotel was refurbished and was reopened in 1962 where the Carrs were joined by Mr and Mrs Derek Carr before selling to Chef and Brewer (part of Grand Met group) in 1968. Until 1972 it was used as a staff-training centre before being used as a hotel again. The freehold was sold in 1978 to meet death duties and then in the early 1980s the hotel was refurbished at a cost of £485,000 and reopened as a Berni Inn.

Royal Exeter Bedroom, 1980s

In 2000 Scottish and Newcastle Breweries, having bought it in 1993, sold it to an independent operator Peter Brewer. It is still an important hotel in the town with restaurants and bars including the 1812 Bar and Bar So.

The number of large Victorian villas that could be divided or extended to become hotels reflected Bournemouth's accommodation. On the West Cliff large boarding houses were created from separate terrace properties such as The Glendevon in West Hill Road, Crag Hall in Durley Gardens (now flats) and Eaglescliffe in Durley Gardens (now also flats).

Crag Hall, 1939

In 1881 The Durley Dean Hotel was still a house owned by Thomas Rawlins, a solicitor, before a new building occupying 3 sides of the square of Durley Gardens was erected in 1904. By 1911 it was known as the Durley Dean Hydro. In the *1913 Bournemouth Guide* it was the Durley Dean Mansions Hotel and Hydro "luxuriously furnished on the bracing West Cliff, the healthiest position in Bournemouth with farm produce supplied by its own farm and having the most up to date hydro in the South of England offering Turkish, Russian and sea water swimming baths. There are two hundred rooms an electric passenger lift and the hydro motorbus will meet any train on receipt of a post card."

By 1969 it advertised: "attractive Cocktail Bar, Bridge Club, Social Hostess, Licensed Ballroom with Maple Dance Floor. Children have no roads to cross, a claim that can be made by few hotels in the district." By 2006, as part of Swallow Hotels, it was in the hands of the receiver. Folio Hotels spent £3 million refurbishing the building including £1 million on the bedrooms and £1 million on the infrastructure including new boilers, and the rest on the bars and conference facilities to attract business customers. However due to high fixed costs and the competition from the budget hotels, shortly after reopening in 2008 the receiver was called in. The hotel had a management buy-out in January 2009.

The Lounge Durley Mansions, 1915

Durley Mansions, 1905

The now Bournemouth Highcliff Marriott Hotel was originally to have been four large houses but as they were being built (around 1873) a company was formed to open a hotel instead. Some of the original building can be seen in the nine bays west of the hotel's entrance. The four houses were divided into two parts. Number 1 was for families and gentlemen on pensions and Number 2 was available as private suites and apartments. The owner John Kilner lived in the property 'Highcliffe Mansions' and the hotel opened for its first guests on 12th December 1874. (Mr Kilner also continued to run 'Osborne' private and high class boarding house in Priory Road for a number of years.) The hotel proved to be very successful and attracted a number of well-to-do guests including Robert Louis Stevenson. Its position on the cliff top gave it both extensive inland and sea views. However in November 1875 Mr Kilner decided to amalgamate the two parts and form a 50-bedroom hotel, changing its name to Highcliffe Mansions Hotel.

Highcliffe Hotel

The *1890 Brights Guide* advertised the hotel's "magnificent sea views, public drawing, reading, coffee, smoking and billiards rooms. Electric light, suites of apartments most private and comfortable. With supplies from our own Alderney Dairy farm." By 1895 it was listed to a Maria Kilner on the Burgess Register.

In 1902 John Steinbridge took over as manager of the Highcliffe Hotel and stayed there until 1940. During this time the hotel expanded considerably, taking over neighbouring properties including, in 1925, nine former Coastguard cottages. A large extension was also built east of the hotel giving it a 500ft sea frontage. By 1948 A&J Wild were the mangers (late of Continental-Savoy and Mena House, Cairo, Baur au Lac, Zurich and Gallia Palace, Cannes) of the 120 roomed hotel, "Many with private baths", "Modern garage" and "Telephones all rooms". On Auguste Wild's death his son Robert took over. In 1956 the hotel's name changed to Highcliff after the Bournemouth hotel lost the "e" on the toss of the coin to Highcliffe Hotel in Highcliffe.

In 1988 the new owners Eldridge Pope added the neighbouring Mon Ami Hotel (previously Glenroy Hall). £4 million was spent creating conference suites, a brasserie and extra bedrooms and linking it all to the main part of the hotel. It became Swallow Highcliff Hotel in 1990 and was bought by Whitbread in 1999 and the name altered to Bournemouth Highcliff Marriott Hotel. In 2007 it was sold to an Irish investment consortium.

Glenroy Hall Hotel, 1930s

Another property developer Robert Kerley who came from a local farming family was arranging land purchases with John Tregonwell, William Clapcott Dean and the Branksome Estate. In 1859 he agreed to build 10 "detached and substantial brick houses of first class character" within 10 years. He also rented Priory Stables probably originally used for Tregonwell's House, The Mansion. Kerley was given permission to build any number of houses within 20 years. The first house he built in Priory Road (named after a small estate in Priory, Devon belonging to Tregonwell's first wife) in 1864 was Sunnyside. Next door he built The Priory, which he himself lived in. After Kerley's death in 1872 it became a boarding house, The Priory Hotel using Sunnyside as an annex. In

1948 it became a Southern Electricity Board office before the Council bought it in 1972 when it was pulled down to make more parking spaces for the Winter Gardens. It is still a car park.

Priory Road, early 1900s

Osborne Hotel, 1928

In 1867 at the bottom of the hill facing Exeter Road two semi-detached houses were built known as Osborne House 1 and 2. By 1874 The Osborne was a boarding house offering 51 bedrooms. The owner Joseph Dines advertised that all the rooms and passages were heated with warn water keeping an even temperature of 60 degrees. It was connected to Dunedin built in 1869 (next door to the Winterbourne.) In 1888 it was advertised as having lofty and spacious rooms and connected with the Osborne by "a fine corridor".

Later Dunedin was separated and became The Georgian Private Hotel before being demolished in 1981 for the BIC car park entrance.

Georgian Hotel, 1928

In 1866 Robert Kerley built a house, which he called Winterbourne, for a retired clergyman Rev Leybourne Popham. It remained home to his spinster daughter until 1925. It was later to become the home of Admiral Grey. In 1932 the lease was granted to J Winkley who converted it into a hotel and extended it. It was demolished in 2005 after plans had been passed to build a large 4-star training hotel.

Next door Upton had become a nursing home for consumptives until the 1920s when it was Abbey Mount Hotel. On the corner of Beacon Road, Abbey Mount and Sandringham Hotel (once Ottershaw House) were connected to form Bournemouth International Hotel. The stables were converted into Ottershaw Garage before being demolished in the 1980s and the Ocean Palace restaurant built.

Winterbourne Hotel, 1948

"OTTERSHAW,"
PRIORY ROAD,
BOURNEMOUTH

'PHONE 280.

PROPRIETORS:
Mr. & Mrs. Taverner

Ottershaw, 1926

On the opposite corner was West Cliff Tower, which was called Durlestone Boarding house in the 1880s. It had a tower built in 1890s and a new front door opening onto Beacon Road. *An Illustrated Guide to Bournemouth* in 1893 advertised it as being: "approached by a well gravelled drive. The sanitary arrangements throughout the house are as perfect as science can make them, and, in fact the Durlestone is just the place to go if you are out of health, and rest and quietude are the restoratives you need." It is now the Bourne Beat Hotel.

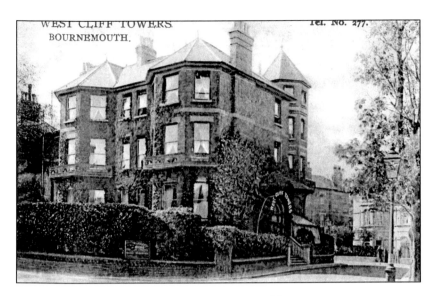

West Cliff Towers, 1938

Next door was West Cliff Hall, built in the 1880s. In the 1890s it was apartments run by the Candy family until the 1920s. It is now called Bourne Hall Hotel. Opposite was Fairmount on the corner of Tregonwell Road built in 1876 and still has its original name. In 1890 it was the home of Harriett Harley.

West Cliff Hall Hotel, 1974

48

A curved road was built by a Mark Carpenter behind the Coastguard cottages and named after Robert Kerley. Woodstock is the present day Marlins Hotel (previously called To The Manor Bourne) and Montgomery House is Brooklands Hotel (formerly Chiselhurst Grange Hotel). The present day Balmoral Hotel was originally called Glenfinnan. In 1896 it was a high-class boarding house called Beacon Royal. In the 1931 guide Mrs James mentions its new wing with service flats, gas fires in bedrooms, central heating, ballroom, table tennis, croquet and amusements arranged. The Mayfield next door was later absorbed into the hotel. Another smaller house, Beaconsfield, was later known as West Cliff Court Hotel and is now known as The Surfer. (In 1923 it was called Allington Grange, owned by Mr and Mrs T. Gunn and advertised as "An ideal Private Hotel".)

South Mount, 1939

On Priory Road villas were built in 1872. Penmellyn (Garthlands from 1881, a boarding house by the 1920s) and St Margarets. St Margarets was bought by Dan Godfrey (the celebrated conductor of Bournemouth Municipal Orchestra) in 1903. He moved out after the First World War and bought Rosstrevor. By the 1920s St Margarets was also a boarding house but now called The Trouville. In 1928 the Polokoffs bought the Trouville and build a new façade. In 1932 they joined it with Garthlands and three years later added a further storey over both properties. In 1960 the owner of the Trouville, Mr Green bought South Mount Hotel (St Regulus) to make more room for garages, 24 bedrooms, a billiard room and extended dining room. The site of South Mount is now the car park for the Trouville. In 1965 The Trouville advertised: "Gala Dances, First Class Cuisine and Courteous Service". The 80 bedroomed hotel had 60 with private bathrooms en-suite all with radio, telephone and razor points. It was "All seasons, inexpensive luxury holiday or honeymoon".

Mrs Kerley had Hylands built (later it was called Highlands and is now the Westcliff Sands Hotel) and it remains fairly unaltered. It was home to Mary Martha Hudson in 1891. In 1931 it was run by Miss Martin and highly recommended for good cooking. In 1969 bedrooms still had gas and electric fires as central heating was only in the public rooms. Terms were 9-15½ guineas for full board.

More houses were built next door; Rosstrevor (1874) and Audley (1876) later called Blenheim and in the 1950s Peel Court. They were joined in 1964 and enlarged in 1979 when Mr Pullinger moved from the Collingwood Hotel in Kerley Road and brought that name with him. More building work was done including adding a mansard roof in 1988.

Peel Court Hotel, 1940s

Before 1880 Tregonwell Road was called Victoria Road. Villas built there are still in evidence with Highclere now Bonnington Beach (formerly Rochdale in 1950 then The Bonnington), Carisbrooke, Moseley Dine (now the Pinedale), The Hollies (now Inverness Hotel), the former Welsh Knoll (now the Mt. Stuart Hotel) and Howrah (now Tregonholme Hotel). In 1969 the tariff for the Tregonholme Hotel was £11-£15 and "based on the Modern Trend of Room, Breakfast and 5-course Dinner".

In the *Bournemouth Guide for 1923* The Pinedale run by Mr and Mrs Meadows advertised, "No efforts are spared to ensure the comfort and convenience of visitors. Excellent cuisine, separate tables and gas fires in bedrooms." In 1969 "The comfortable bedrooms are all close carpeted, with modern furnishings, heating, spring interior mattresses. No attics or basements. Charming lounge with TV."

Letter from Kathleen Wellesley

It had previously been recommended by Kathleen Wellesley, wife of Arthur Wellesley 4th Duke of Wellington, in a letter to Mrs Newlyn.

Two semi-detached houses Wolseley Villas, further down the road, became the Kenilworth Hotel. The Carisbrooke was in the 1920 *Bournemouth Guide* a "select apartment house" with large well furnished rooms, good cooking hot and cold baths, electric light and the house "warmed for extreme weather". In 1969 it was a "modernised hotel offering every comfort and first class cuisine" with Mr and Mrs Ingledew assuring "a happy holiday here".

Many smaller boarding houses were found in the horseshoe shaped roads of St Michaels and Purbeck. In 1902 Mrs Wood offered private apartments at moderate terms at the Newark with board if required. In 1969 there were "special terms for old age pensioners and children from 10 years of age if sharing parents' room". (Presumably they meant children sharing a room with their parents and not the pensioners!)

In 1911 Mrs White at 53 St Michaels Road offered two sitting rooms and four large airy rooms and by 1920 she offered furnished apartments calling it

The Lewisham. The Redlands (Now the Topaz) in St Michaels Road offered board residence with every home comfort. Miss Sears did also stipulate in the *Bournemouth Guide* of 1911 "This home is conducted on Christian Principles. Morning prayers at 9.15 when all will be welcome. Non alcoholic beverage may be used for meals."

Carisbrooke, 1968

Maisoneuve at 57 St Michaels Road offered superior boarding pension at 2½ guineas in 1920. At the Shirley in 1913 Mr and Mrs Barton offered home comforts from 1½-2 guineas according to the room and season. In 1923 Mrs Turpie at Bradgate, 77 St. Michaels Road, (near the Malvern) advertised good cooking, every comfort, and electric light throughout with meals served at separate tables. In 1928 The Beeches (now The Safari) offered "Superior Private Apartments" under "the immediate supervision" of the proprietress Mrs Evens. In the 1969 guide Mr and Mrs Orchard offered, "Good food expertly cooked and well served at separate tables. Drive in free parking."

In the 1950s bed and breakfast was also to be found at nearly every house in St Michaels Road, at No. 32 Richmond, No. 34 Dale Guest House, No. 36 Shalford, No. 39 Laburnum, No. 41 Bycliff, No. 42 Lynbrook, No. 46 Rosedale, No. 48 Rothbourne "Small Select Guest House", No. 52 Fleetwood, No. 54 Croydon with "no petty restrictions", No. 57 Holmlea, No. 59 The

Hilton "All food is prepared by Mrs M. Evans (Diploma Domestic Science)", No. 61 Cremona with its own billiards room, No. 63 Braemar "for good food and a happy holiday", and No. 65 Newark: "Highly recommended for Liberal and Varied Cuisine. Free parking spaces."

The Beeches, 1976

Larger hotels such as The Manchester had: "Large lounges, Writing Rooms, Ballroom. Billiards and Snooker Tables."

The Manchester Hotel

Bedroom, Dining Room and Lounge, Manchester Hotel, 1930s

Mae-Mar, 1962

Connaught Court, 1927

The Glenroy Hall Hotel at the sea end of the road had 100 bedrooms and an "Orchestra during the Season". (It was later to become part of the Highcliff.)

West Hill Road for a number of years had a number of boarding houses such as Arley Glen at No. 111, which Mr and Mrs Potter advertised in the

1924 guide as being "charmingly situated in best part of West Cliff … up to date furnishings … designed to give every comfort from 3gns per week." Bourne View Hotel at No. 55 West Hill Road in 1949 for 6-6½ guineas. "The comfort of guest is first consideration of the proprietress Mrs E. Warden", Hollyhurst "Overlooking the Sea", Mae-Mar "in the heart of the West Cliff Hotel area", West Leigh, No. 65 Windermere, Venn Leigh, West Lynne, No. 83 Bay-Brook, Lancastria, No. 67 St Aubin's Guest House, Brandon, No. 121 West Hill Court Hotel, No. 125 Ulundi Private Hotel, Glendevon where: "A Resident Band plays for Weekly Dances; also other Dances to Radiogram", Connaught Court where: "Set in an acre of grounds this modern Hotel offers all you could wish for in comfort and cuisine."

Bournemouth from the West Cliff, 1910s

Bournemouth at War 1914 - 1918

The holiday season in 1914 stated well with the Easter period having bright and sunny weather with excursion trains bringing a rush of people on 9th April. It was reported over 30,000 people strode along the promenade that weekend.

"As far as Bournemouth was concerned the black clouds of war which were starting to appear over the continent did not exist. The town settled down anticipating a bumper year."(*Bournemouth Guardian*)

Britain declared war on Germany on 4th August 1914 and the crowds that August Bank Holiday were not as large as at Easter. Visitors had returned home early and others had cancelled their bookings. The town clerk dismayed by rumours that Bournemouth was under siege issued a letter to newspapers and all the hotels in the town pointing out that conditions were normal. Slowly visitors started to return.

Crag Head

On 14th August the Defence of the Realm Act 1914 did not allow any person of German nationality to remain without first having a special permit from the police. All aliens were to register at Law Courts and then they were asked to leave. This caused problems in Bournemouth as around 1,200-1,300 aliens worked in the hotels.

The War Office asked Bournemouth to provide accommodation for wounded and sick soldiers; this included the former Royal residence Crag Head which became an emergency hospital.

The summer season in 1915 was not as busy as usual mainly due to the cutbacks in excursions and lack of cheap train tickets. On the promenade it was predominately the wounded who sat out in the sun rather than visitors. The paddle steamer trips were no longer available and so visitors took to driving inland to the New Forest and parts of Dorset.

The hotels were busy for Easter 1916 although there were few Easter eggs or hot cross buns. By the end of August 1916 the charabanc trips ended due to petrol rationing and there was no provision made for pleasure motoring. Christmas was busy for the large hotels but not so good for the smaller establishments.

Bournemouth continued to try and retain a happy holiday atmosphere for the war-weary soldiers and Whitsun 1917 (there had been no Whitsun holiday in 1916) saw Bournemouth as the busiest resort in the country despite the heavy rain.

The hotels were busy at Whitsun 1918 but the seafront was filled with wounded and convalescent servicemen.

Annerley Court, 1953

An incident at 4 p.m. on 22nd July 1918 took place by two hotels: The Southcombe (now called The Water Gardens) and Arundale Hotel Court (called Annerley Court Hotel in the 1950s and renamed Palm Court in 1997 and now Ocean City Chinese restaurant) on the corner of Annerley and Christchurch Road. Major John Locock the pilot and Captain PG Bridgewood an observer were flying a Bristol fighter at 100mph when the aircraft struck the top of a tree before touching live tram wires, plunging the plane to the ground and killing the pilot. Eyewitnesses said it was flying too low as the pilot had been supposedly buzzing the house of his girlfriend. Low flying in built up areas was banned shortly afterwards.

Southcombe Hotel

After the war ended in November 1918 the hotels found bookings at Christmas were back to the pre-war scale.

Between the Wars

The 1919 holiday season was great success and the beaches packed despite some mines having been washed up. One of the main attractions for visitors was the German submarine U-107 at Poole Quay. Around 10,000 visitors raised £700 for the King's fund for disabled officers and men.

Annual events that had been suspended during the war were reinstated including lawn tennis, croquet, and cricket week. The rail strike in September 1919 however made it difficult for holidaymakers and some cut short their stays. Charabancs were laid on to London, Bristol, Birmingham and Bath and The Square was full with holidaymakers and their luggage.

THE WEST CLIFF, BOURNEMOUTH.

Looking towards the West Cliff, 1927

The town made the most of telling potential visitors of its activities. In the children's corner in the Lower Pleasure Gardens children could sail boats on the Bourne Stream. On the beach alongside beach bungalows and tents, family or mixed sea bathing was allowed under *proper restrictions*! There were steamer excursions to Swanage, the Isle of Wight, Southampton and Southsea, river boating on the River Stour at Tuckton and Iford. Motor coaches went daily to places of interest and beauty such as Corfe, Salisbury, Stonehenge or the New Forest. There was cycling, the Natural Science Society, rambles, golf, cricket, football, hockey, bowls, tennis, croquet, fishing, yachting, the theatre, cinema and a skating rink. For those still not sure the "purity of water supply, high standard of its sanitation and exceptional cleanliness of streets are reflected in death rates which is lowest of all the large towns in England." The guide was also proud to point out the absence of slums!

The regatta was restored in 1920 and the "submarine flying boat rides very popular". Bournemouth was back in business! It seemed people were returning to their old haunts after the war, although holidays by the sea were still affected by the weather. According to the 1927 guide: "The old prejudice against Bournemouth that because it is relatively warm in winter it must therefore be hot and oppressive in summer still lingers, but it is rapidly being dispelled by the experience of those who find that on the cliffs and stealing through the Chines there are always refreshing sea breezes, mingling with the scent of the pines."

Grand Hotel, 1925

The First World War had however seen a huge increase in death duties to be paid. The Government brought in The Finance Act of 1919 to help pay for the cost of the war. The Dean Estates had to find 26% death duty. It was a huge amount and with inflation reducing real income from ground rents and with costs rising, the only answer was to sell some freeholds.

May 1921 saw the auction of the freeholds of many properties including ones from the Meyrick Estate such as Brookside, Southcliffe Hall (formerly

Nos. 3 & 4 Cliftonville); Vale Royal, Meyrick Cliffs, Westminster Hall Hotel in Beacon Road; Belvedere and The Grand Hotel in Firvale Road which had 30 staff bedrooms, 91 bedrooms and stood in 2¾ acres. Ground rent was £80 p.a. on a 99-year lease from 1894 but there was an extra £20 p.a. added to the rent from 1898 when Mr Dore and Mr Preston made alterations to the premises. It was renovated between 1893 and 1905. The hotel had originally been built in 1861 on the site of an old house. (In 1855 the road was known as Church Glen and had a stream that ran from a pond in Horseshoe Common down a deep ravine near to where the Department store Dingles is today.) In 1882 the house was converted into the Grand Firvale Hotel, later known just as The Grand, before being closed in 1960 and demolished in 1962.

Meyrick Mansion and Meyrick Lodge opposite the Royal Bath Hotel (formerly The County Hotel and now Prezzo and unfinished flats) had a proviso that Bournemouth Corporation proposed to widen Westover and Hinton Roads and strips of land would have to be surrendered but the rent would not be reduced! In the 1927 guide Meyrick Mansion was advertised as Hotel de Luxe with hot air radiators controlled at visitors' will. They however also stated, "For the safety and pleasure of Visitors to the hotel the Management begs to say that no infectious or consumptive cases are received."

Meyrick Mansions, 1930

The Westover Villas built in 1836-1839 in Westover Road were pulled down by property developers and the land used for building a huge cinema. The Regent Theatre's entrance hall was paved in black and white marble and there were café/restaurant and lounges. It was renamed The Gaumont in 1949 and then the Odeon in 1968.

The Square, 1930

A new luxury hotel the Palace Court Hotel (now Premier Inn) was built in white concrete and opened in 1936. The Palace Court was intended to look like a liner and was the epitome of 1930s sophistication. It had its own theatre, hairdresser, outfitters, restaurants and cocktail bar. In 1938, from January to October, it had 20,800 visitors. (It was bought by the Littman family in 1948 and in 1968 was given a £100,000 face-lift. In 1988 Classic Hotels bought it for £6 million, selling it to the Stakis group in 1994 for £7.6 million. It then became part of the Hilton umbrella for Ladbrokes until 2005 when it traded as Metro Hotel before being sold to Golden Tulip who, whilst renovating it, were bought by Premier Inn.)

Meyrick Court

In 1929 The New Meyrick Court was opening on the corner of Christchurch Road and Derby Road as the old hotel on the Bath Road had been demolished for road widening. The hotel had a lift, hot and cold running water, gas fires, central heating and was "modern to a degree". It later became holiday flats (Ocean Court).

Barton (later known as the Knightlow Hotel) in Percy Road, Boscombe, was typical in advertising itself as a comfortable board residence with cleanliness and good food a speciality. (In December 1895 sites had been sold from the Boscombe Manor Estate including plots in Percy Road and Michelgrove Road.)

Tower Mansions (later Byng Mansions then Carlton Court, Christchurch Road, Boscombe), in 1920, was one of a few hotels which boasted that the food was from their own farm.

Byng Mansions, 1981

The Belvedere in Bath Road was described as: "A well known and high class Boarding Establishment in a most convenient position quite close to the East Cliff, Pier and Centre of town." Its neighbour Red Roofs was a private residence with 11 bedrooms and a lease of 99 years from 1899 for £10 p.a. and later became a hotel trading under this name until it was changed to The Grosvenor; it is now part of the Belvedere.

Redroofs Hotel, 1930s

Hotels in areas of Bournemouth such as Terrace Mount had their heyday in the 1920s and 1930s. They had reasonably priced accommodation, sea views and as most people came by train the lack of parking was not an issue. The 1920s-1930s were a boom time for the working classes' holidays. 1n 1933, 53 coaches ran from 19 towns in Lancashire to Bournemouth. By 1935, 799 coaches came from 190 towns to the resort. However The Depression in the 1930s affected the financial situation of many people, particularly badly hit were those from the industrial towns in northern England and the holiday trade changed with some people reducing their normal 2 week break to just 1 week.

Growing up in the town at this time was Tony Hancock. His family had moved from Birmingham when he was nearly 3 years old. His father Jack Hancock (a part-time entertainer) took over The Railway Hotel next to the brewery and close to Bournemouth Central Station on Holdenhurst Road. The Railway Hotel is thought to have been built on the site of the brickworks that builder David Tuck rented from Sir George Meyrick Tapps. The hotel was demolished in 1973 and replaced by an office block by St Paul's roundabout. After a row with his employers, Jack Hancock moved his family in August 1933 to the Swanmore and Lodge Hotel at 3 Gervis Road East. Although the small hotel was neglected, it was in a more upmarket area with tree lined wide pavements and close to the sea. The hotel was renamed the Durlston Court in 1934 after the preparatory boarding school Colin and later Tony attended.

By 1935 the hotel had been completely rebuilt as a much larger, ultra modern building. A feature in *The Bournemouth Daily Echo* August 7 1935 reveals that it was designed and built by a local company (Rowley and Company of Bush House, Lansdowne.) It had central heating throughout, electric fires and hot and cold water in every bedroom. "The beautiful Gardens (designed and laid out by Mr W. A. Walton) enhance a dignified example of modern architecture. The profusion of the lawns contrasts pleasantly with the strong white surface of the building."

The hotel was busy with its theatrical and show business customers and in 1935 had bookings from all 3 summer shows and touring companies. Jack Hancock was a popular landlord and entertainer and would have his family and guests in fits of laughter with his anecdotes and jokes.

However on 11th August 1935, Jack Hancock died from cancer and peritonitis. Tony was 11 years old. The ambience of the hotel changed to one of more gentle folk.

Swanmore, 1930

Hancock enjoyed watching the old ladies who tended to be permanent residents. He joked they would set out for the dining room at 11.30 a.m. and get there just in time for the gong at one o'clock! Hancock would write out menus for his mother inventing names for the dishes such as 'Potage Luxembourg'. His mother did remark that, "Tony once asked me why he couldn't have a home life like other boys. But it was impossible of course I was busy with customers all the time." On 1st January 1936 Tony's mother married Bournemouth and Boscombe footballer Robert Walker. It is possible they met when his company installed the electrics for the new hotel. Tony's mother ran the hotel with his brother Colin until the war. By 1947 the hotel was under the ownership of Mr and Mrs T Fraser. After leaving school Tony Hancock drifted from job to job until he was sent to the Carlton Hotel where he worked as a clerk.

However, Tony appeared to have inherited his father's talent to work in entertainment and, although his first major engagement as a comic did not go down too well at the local Catholic Hall, he joined the RAF in 1942 where he took part in the Gang Shows until 1946. After his death it was found he had left all his property to his mother Mrs Lucie Sennett of Redroofs Hotel where she lived.

ELSTEAD PRIVATE HOTEL,
Knyveton Road,
Telephone : 2829.   **Bournemouth**
Telegrams : Shaw, 2829 Bournemouth.
Proprietors—Mr. & Mrs. Shaw.

Elstead Hotel 1920s
(The name changed frequently between Elstead and Elsteade during the 1920s and 1930s)

However hotels like The Elsteade (now The Elstead) in Knyveton Road had expanded and extolled people to: "Come as strangers – go as friends." "For 1934 Its Elsteade – search no more." They enthused in the 1934 *Bournemouth Guide* about the hotel's virtues. "Liberal Fare is daintily served. Special diets are willingly studied." "First class ping pong table, all electric gramophone and wireless set." In 1940 it was "The Positive Pole of Magnetic Bournemouth."

The local Hotel Association published a letter it had received in its magazine: "Would any member be prepared to offer accommodation in a double room with two beds in exchange for a 1934 Ford Ten motor car?" Unfortunately they do not follow up on the outcome! They had far more serious issues because in the summer of 1936 disaster hit Bournemouth. The town experienced the worst milk-borne typhoid epidemic this country has ever known. In July 1936 a small dairy farmer unknowingly delivered his infected milk to Frowds Dairy. The source of contamination was eventually traced to Captain Hambro of Merley House, MP for Dorset. At the dairy other milk was collected and pooled thus infecting all the milk.

Crowds swelled the numbers in the town for the August Bank holiday. People started reporting signs of food poisoning symptoms but nothing was seen as being serious as the disease has a ten to fourteen day incubation period and early symptoms are vague. By 20th August 315 people locally had visited doctors and the Ministry of Health was called in. The couple that ran Russell Court Hotel lost their son Ken Turley to typhoid. His death was one of around 70 out of 718 reported cases. The milk from Frowds Dairy was identified as the common factor and the milk was immediately pasteurised.

The town's reputation was of a prosperous healthy holiday resort and Bournemouth feared an infectious disease hitting the tourist trade as had happened to Brighton in 1929. Great efforts were made to reduce rumours and reassure the public that drinking water and sea bathing was safe. Unlike many newspapers today the media were not alarmist. The local paper knew the town's reputation was at stake and was urged to avoid emotive articles. However the hotels did see a decline and traders agreed not to press for payments until the holiday trade recovered.

To boost public confidence in Bournemouth, later that year, the *Daily Echo* announced, "The Corporation are building a new swimming bath and health baths costing £76,000." The swimming pool and baths including Turkish, brine and seawater were completed in 1937 and the south side could be opened onto the sun terrace. (Now the site of the Waterfront and controversial Imax building.)

As the town recovered the Official Information Bureau published their new guide *Bournemouth Britain's All-Seasons Resort Official guide 1939-1940*. It was a hard backed book complete with colour photographs. The foreword by Mayor Dickinson is still as relevant today: "The holiday-makers demands generally speaking are too comprehensive to be satisfied by natural beauty alone, and recognising this the town council, very ably supported by other interests in the town, has promoted entertainment and recreational facilities which are outstanding in this country and, in fact, in some respects have been acclaimed to be unrivalled anywhere in the world."

Visitors to Bournemouth had an incredible choice of entertainment. The Pavilion built at a cost of £300,000 housed a concert hall, a ballroom and restaurants. Highly successful actors brought West End plays; the Bournemouth Municipal Orchestra (largest of its kind in the world) gave six performances a week plus open-air concerts in Pine Walk. There were three other theatres and variety halls, 16 cinemas, an ice rink, new indoor swimming pool with aquatic shows. Concert parties took place at the beach at Boscombe and open-air dancing on Bournemouth Pier. Shops included Harvey Nicholls in Commercial Road which advertised in the *Residential Bournemouth Book* as having: "Several spacious showrooms in which you are cordially invited to inspect a fine collection of modern and reproduction furniture, British and Oriental carpets and fine furnishings."

For the more sports-minded there were two municipal 18 hole golf courses, tennis courts, putting, bowls (a new indoor bowling green was opened in November 1937 on the site of the Winter Gardens), cricket, boating, fishing, croquet and hunting.

EAST PROMENADE FROM BOURNEMOUTH PIER.

Pier Approach Baths

The hundreds of hotels, guesthouses and bed and breakfast establishments to be found in the 1939 guide looked forward to a prosperous season. The Marsham Court (the name is said to have originated from the owners Mr and Mrs Marsh who had a ham business) had 110 rooms and an average number of 134 visitors per day for the previous 12 months. They boasted all beds were fitted with a special make of spring mattress, rooms had bedside reading lamps and there was a ballroom with special coloured lighting effects.

The Marsham Court

The Marsham Court had been the first hotel to have hot and cold water in the bedrooms. A year later the hotel was the American Red Cross headquarters and the HQ for the land registry and issuing instructions to only use the nightlights provided in an emergency, as they were difficult to obtain.

The Lounge Ballroom, Marsham Court

Bournemouth at War 1939 - 1945

On the 3rd September 1939 Britain declared war on Germany. The number of visitors in Bournemouth fell by about 10% with the smaller hotels and boarding houses suffering the most. The cinemas, theatres and other places of entertainment were closed but two weeks later they were reopened and by the end of November audiences were back at pre-war levels. By Christmas bookings had returned to normal. 3,000 copies of a winter poster had been placed in railway stations which must have helped trade although the number of trains to Bournemouth had been cut from 14 to 6 a day. Services did improve for Christmas and shows including *No No Nanette* at the Pavilion and *Robinson Crusoe* at the Boscombe Hippodrome (later the Opera House, now O² Academy Bournemouth) did well. Hotels were advised not to reduce prices as some visitors had been going from hotel to hotel bemoaning the extra income tax they had to pay. The Hotel Association warned that with prices rising such as gas up by 25%, meat, sugar, butter and fish up by 20-40% it would be suicidal to cut rates.

The late Sunday evening church service for hoteliers and their staff that had been arranged earlier in 1939 was withdrawn due to the blackout. Public transport was provided by the electrically powered trolley buses, which finished at 9.30 p.m. Their windows were covered over and with the lack of street lighting the blackout made it difficult to get around at night.

Warden posts were set up all over the town including one at Five Ways Hotel, 423 Charminster Road, Winton. The hotel also had a public shelter for 30 people. Meanwhile many hotels had converted their basements to air raid shelters. The Grand Hotel used its garage for a shelter to accommodate 150 people with bunks for 30 people. The Strouden Park Hotel, Castle Lane (now under Castlepoint Shopping Centre) could accommodate 47 in its basement shelter. The Hotel Association reported that 200 hotelkeepers had completed the ARP course. The wardens would call on hoteliers after evening meals were finished to come and help.

By March 1940 road and rail travel was normal and thousands of visitors headed for the resort. The Whitsun Bank Holiday was cancelled but those who had booked still came. They couldn't fail to notice the machine guns on the top of the Town Hall, Beales and Highcliff Hotel. The hotels and boarding houses were visited to check for restricted "aliens" and 100 people were taken away. The Mayor W Hayward wrote in the guide: "Our country is at war. In days between 1914-1918 Bournemouth's privilege as a health and pleasure resort was to fill an important place in the national effort. The wounded found here health and recreation and the war-weary a place of leisure and quiet where strength was restored. Today Bournemouth is once again called upon to play her part and offers to those on whom the stress of present conditions bears heavy, health and pleasure provided by unrivalled facilities for entertainment and recreation. This message is written in time of war; it is my fervent hope that it may be read in time of peace." The 1940 guide is full of hotels advertising with some such as The Cottonwood run by Mr and Mrs Scoular completely ignoring the war. "Standing in its own grounds and commanding one of the finest and healthiest positions on the East Cliff with full view of the entire bay. All beds fitted with interior spring mattresses specially made for the hotel. Bathing bungalow situated in nicest part of beach. From 4gns per week."

Cottonwood, 1927

The Heathlands meanwhile mentioned that their air raid shelter accommodated 100 people. The Suncliff: "Sheltered on the north by pine woods every particle of sun is trapped and the cold winds barred", "Ultra violet ray sun lounge" with "Sunshine day and night" and "Hot sea water baths no charge".

In May 1940 the Labour Party's National Executive Committee met at the Highcliffe Hotel and informed Downing Street that they would join a National

72

Government but not with Chamberlain as Prime Minister. Hours later Winston Churchill was sent for to form a Government. After the war The Highcliffe reopened on May 20th 1946 with the Labour Party Conference. Terms for the week on full board were 9 guineas.

Easter 1941 saw hotels open but the beach was not accessible although there were deckchairs on the promenade and in the gardens, but no music. Factory workers had not been given time off so there were few holidaymakers. Bombs were dropped on the town on Maundy Thursday, 10th April, and again on 12th April with one bomb landing in the garden of the Royal Exeter Hotel.

The Palace Court Hotel was an observation post for the Fire Brigade to direct the appliances to bombed areas. They also advertised in the 1940 guide as: "The building is fireproof and has an anti-gas refuge 15 feet below road level." This was good news indeed as many were perhaps unaware that the garage below the ice rink was being used as a munitions factory with a hundred workers!

Rest centres for bombed out mothers and babies, especially from heavily hit areas such as Bristol, were set up including the Cintra Hotel, Florence Road in Boscombe. This was later transferred to the Studland Dene Hotel in Alum Chine.

Cintra Hotel, 1930

Hawthorns, 1930

The Lounge, Hawthorns Hotel

However by July 1941 people were prevented from entering the South Coast Defence area unless they were on business or residents. Many hotels closed although others were taken over by Government Departments. The Hawthorns (now the Wessex Hotel) had been the home of Fanny Campbell her daughter Marion and 8 servants in 1891. By 1893 the Langley-Taylors were running it as a high-class boarding establishment. They had it enlarged in 1893, 1895 and 1897. Later it was a private hotel "en Pension" advertising the latest Burroughs and Watts full-sized billiard table, good lock-up bicycle room, bathrooms and lavatories on each floor and the house being kept at an even temperature of 60 degrees during the winter by a modern hot water system, built entirely fireproof. Dr J Staple of Bristol remarked in the *Medical Times and Gazette 1895*: "Should any member of the profession contemplate a visit to this lovely spot, he could not do better than make this his headquarters."

The Trouville Hydro (Durley Gardens) and Meyrick Cliffs (Beacon Road, West Cliff) were branches of the Home Office, Aliens, Immigration and Nationality. The Cumberland Hotel was taken over by the Royal Army Pay Corps. The ATS worked at the Cumberland but were billeted at the Picardy Hotel at the corner of Meyrick and Gervis Roads (later known as the Embassy Hotel before being demolished for flats.)

Picardy Hotel, 1960

Hinton Firs in Manor Road was also taken over by the Army Pay Corps and then Canadian Armed Forces. Mr Waters reopened the hotel in 1946 and ran it until his son took over in 1951. It was sold in February 1999 to Mr and Mrs Smith from Melford Hall Hotel, which they had sold for development.

Hinton Firs Hotel, 1930

Hinton Firs Hotel, 1960s

In November 1941 the Anglo Swiss Hotel (called Hotel Royale from 1937-38) was accused of being anti-Semitic in the House of Commons. When the director of the hotel was asked why they did not cater for members of the Semitic race, he replied it was not to prevent Jewish guests (they already had Jewish residents) it was just to inform them that Kosher cooking was not available. The hotel has recently reverted back to the name of Hotel Royale.

The town was becoming used to the forces being present and welcomed them, although the hotels were concerned over the allowances paid. The United Churches National Services Club was established at The Queen Hotel in the Lansdowne, (now Jacey House).

Queen Hotel, 1930

Soldiers were billeted all over the town and the churches opened up for billiards, darts and cards. The Royal Canadian Air Force requisitioned 43 hotels for accommodation. These included Anglo Swiss (in Gervis Road), Royal Bath (in Bath Road), East Cliff Court (East Overcliff Road), Hawthorns (now

Wessex Hotel), Melford Hall (now flats in St Peter's Road. The owner Mr Harry Brown had been in partnership with Mr & Mrs Marsh but opened Melford Hall in 1922. After it was requisitioned he moved to The Savoy Hotel on the West Cliff).

Melford Hall, 1950s

Other hotels taken over were Byng Mansions (opposite Boscombe Chine Gardens), Cottonwood (East Overcliff Road), Carlton (East Overcliff Road), Vale Royal (Punshon House next to the Hermitage), Walmer (in Exeter Gardens), Osborne (in Exeter Road), Burley Court (in Bath Road), Highcliff (now the Marriott), Bourne Dene (in Manor Road and now known as Acacia Hotel).

Walmer Hotel, 1969

Most hotels put their furnishings into store for safekeeping and to make room, as the Canadians brought their own camp beds. Maples had five stores in Bournemouth full of hotel furniture. Also requisitioned was Delamere (1, Rosemount Road Alum Chine), Compton House (billet for ATS), The Grand (in Fir Vale Road); Somerset House in Bath Road was their Post Office. The hotel in 1924 had previously been: "First class apartments with private suites or board residence." The hotel changed its name to New Somerset House in the 1980s, New Concept Lodge in the 1990s and is now called The Mayfair.

Somerset House, 1960

Earls Court (now flats in Gervis Road) was their hospital. (Earls Court built in 1873 was originally called Lindisfarne and in 1897 was the home of Countess Mary Harriett Cairns. In 1921 John Butterworth ran it as a private hotel before changing its name to Earls Court when in 1924 it cost 13/6d per day and offered tennis, garage and stabling. In 1942 it was called St Swithun's Court. It was later converted into flats.)

Others hotels were used as classrooms. The Civilian Technical Corps, who were involved in Radar, had a reception depot at Eglan Court Hotel, Knyveton Road but were accommodated at Annerley Court Hotel (now a Chinese restaurant Ocean City, formerly Arundale Hotel and then Palm Court Hotel).

Gervis Court Hotel in Gervis Road also had servicemen billeted. It was whilst central heating was being put in many years later that letters were found in the floorboards from a woman to one of the men she had met whilst at Burtonwood in Lancashire. There was also a time capsule showing the Christmas entertainment for 1941 where whistling and modelling balloons were part of the programme. Called The Purcells in 1936 it was advertising bed lights, gas fires and rings and an electric iron and pressing board for visitors to use. By 1937 it had lock up garages for 8/6d per week or free parking on the drive and had changed its name to the one it is still known by.

Earls Court, 1928

Gervis Court Hotel

Another hotel that took in transient Canadian airmen was Burley Court on Bath Road. Murray Peden in his book *A Thousand Shall Fall* describes his experiences in Bournemouth. He arrived on 6th December to a town with its beach mined and its access denied by barbed wire. He would walk to the Officers Mess in the Royal Bath Hotel for meals such as powdered egg and spam for breakfast. Eleanor Wolstencroft a young woman at the time remembers the sound of their boots as hundreds of servicemen went for their meals.

Burley Court Hotel, 1957

Parades would take place at 9 a.m. and 1.30 p.m. Peden describes practising crawling into rubber dinghies at the Linden Hall Hydro (Christchurch Road, Boscombe) where although 90 airmen would start the march to the pool only 70 would arrive, many having wandered off. Previously Burley Court in the *1927 Bournemouth Guide* cost four guineas per week and was "beautifully furnished, decorated and equipped with every modern comfort and convenience with garage accommodation within one minute".

An Australian airman Don Charlwood was also stationed in Bournemouth. He wrote about marching through the beautiful town with trainees of the RAF, RCAF and RNZAF and how he exaggerated being Australian. Another airman, Hank Nelson, wrote about meeting English women (over 2,000

Australians married British women). However alcohol was a competitor. Geoffrey Williams, a rear gunner, said that on their six days leave he and friends would go on "a binge of drinking and sex to block out what was behind – and ahead. I'd be almost incoherent for two days after a mission."

On 6th June 1942 the Anglo Swiss hotel took a direct hit from a ME109 hitting the games room and some bedrooms. Three airmen died including 29 year old James Morgan a gunner with the RCAP. They are all buried in War Graves plots in the North Cemetery. Lord Haw Haw warned RCAF that if the airmen looked at the clock in the Anglo Swiss they would see it was 10 minutes slow. The hotel was also later the scene of the rape and murder of Lance Corporal Enid Marion Simpson by Icelandic seaman Astralder Brynjolfsson. He was employed as a civilian by American forces and therefore subject to American military law and was sentenced to life imprisonment.

By 1943 everyday necessities were in short supply and the Board of Trade issued the following statement for visitors: "No coupons can be issued to hotels, boarding houses etc for purchase of towels – You must be prepared to take your towel with you."

On 23rd May 1943, on a fine sunny day, 12 German Focke-Wulf 190 fighter-bombers and 12 Messerschmitt 109s mounted "a low level attack against the port of Bournemouth". (German radio)

Central Hotel, 1927

The Central Hotel built in 1886 on Richmond Hill took a direct hit and was destroyed. (It is believed the hotel was built on waste ground that had previously been excavated into a cave where drinkers gathered to drink alcohol outside of licensed hours.) The bar was crowded with pre-lunch drinkers and diners in the restaurant. Twenty seven were killed, mainly airmen who had arrived the previous day. John Wolstencroft, as part of the Civil Defence, was sent to help. He had just had his own narrow escape when a Messerschmitt attempted to gun him down as he walked from the pier through the gardens. The Central Hotel was too badly damaged to reopen and it was later demolished. The Alliance and Leicester Building Society opened their office on the site in 1953.

A Spitfire shot down a Focke-Wulf 190 and it crashed into St Ives Hotel, 34 Grove Road killing the pilot. The bomb on board didn't explode but the plane caught fire gutting the hotel and killing two people in the hotel next door. Grove Road in the early 1850s had been called Boscombe Grove. Nearby Bath Road had only led as far as the Royal Bath Hotel when it became the Christchurch Road and Russell Cotes Road was Cliff Road.

Hotel Metropole, 1910

The Metropole Hotel in Lansdowne (formerly The Palace Hotel) opened in August 1893 after initially being rejected as encroaching on the highway. It had been the site of Lansdowne House built in 1865 and pulled down around 1890. The Lansdowne name was based on an area in the city of Bath (famous for curative waters). The Metropole Hotel was built by Messrs Red, Blight and Co Ltd of London and Plymouth. It was advertised in 1899 as a "Palatial edifice" with "conveniences of a first class American hotel and all the comforts of a well-conducted English Hotel". It had 120 bedrooms and a beautiful entrance flanked by columns of polished red Aberdeen granite.

In 1943 it was a billet for Canadian, Australian and American airmen. On 23rd May a 500 lb bomb hit the hotel on its Holdenhurst Road side. Walls and floors collapsed killing 12 people. The fire brigade with their new 100ft turntable ladder rescued 35 trapped airmen from the upper floors. One was Eddie Robichaud who for hours was trapped on the 4th floor where he could see bodies crunched up against the chimney and all the way down to the Holdenhurst Road. The Christchurch Road side of the hotel was not as badly damaged. Mr David Gear, aged 76, was in the boiler room where he immediately turned the electricity off and helped damped down the fires. The landlord survived as he had been standing on the stairs. A Mr Spicer who had been sitting in the recess above the entrance remembered the barmaid calling out that she had lost her handbag. Despite all the damage the hotel reopened that September. But in 1950 plans were approved for a new building and in 1955 the site was cleared and the Royal London House opened in 1958.

Pine Court, 1930

The Kingsway Hotel on Lansdowne Road had five staff killed when a bomb went straight through the Baptist Church opposite and into their kitchen. The hotel was a popular place for the Welsh miners who were staying at Court Royal to come for tea and coffee.

In all on that day 77 civilians and 131 military were killed, 196 civilians injured, 22 buildings destroyed with 268 buildings seriously damaged and 3,154 damaged. An American, Lieutenant Thelma Kellgren was down for a quiet weekend break with three friends. Bournemouth was believed to be safe as they had a radar screen and sirens. The planes however had flown under the radar screen and were gone as quickly as they came. The two surgeons and two nurses were in the main street and Kellgren wrote about helping with the wounded in a makeshift casualty station and operating theatre in the ballroom of a large hotel.

Despite the bombing, the hotels had a fairly good summer although only half of the emergency ration cards for visitors had been issued compared to 1942. Pine Court in Gervis Road (an empty hotel and formerly called Leicester House) was the Food Office, Milk Office and National Registration Office. The bank holiday was brisk with visitors watching the military displays and march-pasts.

Heathlands Hotel, East Cliff, Bournemouth.   Telephone Bournemouth 23336

Heathlands Hotel, 1972

Various hotels housed troops including the Black Watch at the Burlington Hotel Boscombe. The Broughty Ferry Hotel (Sea Road, Boscombe, now flats) was the HQ of No. 5 Commando. On getting it back in 1946 the owner Mr Anstee lived in it with his camp bed, using an iron bar to kill the rats. With furniture purchased from the NAAFI and parachute material for furnishings he reopened for business on Christmas Eve 1946. The Miramar (Overcliff Drive) provided accommodation for nurses. Gresham Court, (once known as Neilghewerries, had been a high-class accommodation house in 1908 offering furnished apartments) and Granville Court (now part of Heathlands Hotel both in Gervis Road) billeted WAC officers. It had been the Red Cross Club for US forces but it merged with the clubs from the Trouville and Miramar into one club at the Marsham Court Hotel. (The Granville Hotel was returned to its owners on 10th December 1945 and was full of Christmas guests by 20th December.)

The Tralee was taken over in 1940 by Cox and Kings the army's bankers. (In 1893 it had been the home and shop for Mr William Mattocks but by 1896 it was the only boarding house in the road having extensive sea views.)

Tralee, 1930

Army record offices were housed at Dunholme Manor (pulled down and now flats in Manor Road), Toft House and Coolhurst (in Manor Road).

The American Red Cross held dances at their Officers Club at the Ambassador Hotel (now the Britannia, Meyrick Road), where "young lady residents were invited to entertain American Officers". They however had to fill in a questionnaire to see if they were suitable! It seems the servicemen were also very popular with the residents of Bournemouth especially with organising Christmas parties and presents for local children.

In February 1944 road signs started to be put back after they were removed during the invasion scare in 1940. Later in the year the ban on using the town's name was lifted from shop signs, delivery vans and churches.

In March 1944 there was a ban on all visitors to the South Coast due to the build up of troops and equipment preparing for the invasion of Europe on 6th June. The Chief Superintendent of Police notified all hotel and boarding house keepers to cancel all bookings for visitors who were not exempt and those in residences who were not exempt to leave by 1st April. However the impact was not great as many of the hotels were requisitioned to house soldiers in readiness for the invasion and others who took in guests were already occupied by residents (presumably those who had been bombed out). Servicemen on leave were allowed in the banned area along with children visiting parents.

The Norfolk Hotel, 1940

The Norfolk advertised in the local paper for residents of Bournemouth of the wonderful opportunity to stay at a really first-rate class hotel as visitors were unable to come. (The Norfolk Hotel had originally been two villas numbers 5 & 6 that had been converted into Stewarts Private Hotel. In 1893: "The patrons of the Stewarts are of an eminently high class, embracing many well-known members of the nobility and other distinguished visitors." In 1901-1906 it was Hotel Bristol before becoming Norfolk Hotel in 1907. In the Second World War it was the only fully licensed hotel not to be requisitioned.)

In July 1944 the ban on visitors was lifted and on Bank Holiday Saturday 9,000 people left Waterloo but found the hotels fully booked due to 400 being requisitioned and not yet released. On the 13th October a Londoner wrote to the *Echo* complaining of the lack of hotel accommodation. Bournemouth had a record wartime season and all hotels were full for October.

East Anglia Hotel, 1940s

The Americans made themselves at home by celebrating Thanksgiving at the Marsham Court and Trouville.

Bournemouth Council was planning reconstruction and development of the town for after the war. Bournemouth, Poole and Christchurch commissioned Professor Abercrombie from London to survey and report on possible development of the towns, especially the seafront in Bournemouth. Nothing came from the report.

By April 1945, after a very cold winter, there was a big improvement on the seafront. German POW's had removed barbed wire, stakes, dragon's teeth and anti invasion obstacles. The town was chosen as a leave centre for battle-weary American soldiers and was known as "The Miami of Britain".

By Whitsun weather forecasts were available and people could plan their trips; 19,000 arrived for the holiday by train despite it not being very sunny.

Unbeknown to many people in Bournemouth, an underground headquarters had been built near St Leonards Hotel, Ringwood and used by the Free French and De Gaulle. A few enterprising hoteliers took advantage of the French's ability to procure petrol and offered their services as chauffeurs to all the important visitors. The owner of the Pembroke Hotel (Poole Hill) was given a decoration from the French for his war work.

Glengarry Hotel, 1930

In November 1945, the Americans vacated the Hawthorns, Tollard Royal (West Cliff Promenade which had previously been owned by Mr and Mrs J Butterworth in 1901), Southcliffe, East Cliff Mansions, Trouville, Priory, Granville Court and 'Glengarry', 105 St Michael's Road, which from 1920 had been an annexe of the Highcliffe.

All hotels had been used by the Red Cross and were easy to convert back. The Royal Exeter, Whitehall and Tollard Royal (converted to flats in 1956) had been leave centres for US troops and the Savoy Hotel had been the Artillery Records Office. However hotels used as billets had not been so well treated. One hotelier found that his rooms had been used to train night fighter pilots and had been painted with black tar!

In September 1945, 90 hotels were still occupied by the War Department. By December this had dropped to 76 and by February 1946 only 20 remained occupied.

By Easter 1946, 150 hotels had been handed back to their owners. The repatriation of the RCAF meant 43 hotels were vacated by 1st March apart from The Grand and Compton House. At any one time 12,000 Canadians were billeted in Bournemouth.

The Carlton Hotel had been taken over in 1940 by the Board of Trade with departments for the rationing of clothes and petrol. The hotel was also home to The American Bureau of Investigation. In 1944 Generals Eisenhower and Montgomery stayed at the hotel to discuss operational tactics for the Normandy landings and watched rehearsals in the bay. By January 1946 the Carlton was used to house GI brides; 213 wives and 224 children left for Southampton and sailed on the Queen Mary to their new lives.

Another Suite, called the WESTMINSTER, furnished in the Sheraton style, and consists of two or more Bedrooms as desired, all having access to the FINEST MARINE BALCONY in Bournemouth.

Many of the Bedrooms communicate by double doors and open to BALCONIES overlooking the SEA.

In order to provide accommodation for an increasing number of Visitors, a Villa has been erected in the Grounds and this contains several good size Bedrooms with south-west aspect.

A CORNER OF THE DRAWING ROOM

The CARLTON is under the experienced management of MRS. TRIGG, formerly of the Thackeray Hotel, London.

Good STABLING and a MOTOR GARAGE are provided for Visitors.

The Omnibus meets trains at either Railway Station by appointment, and is available to take parties to the Theatre, Winter Gardens, Dances, etc.

The Carlton Hotel, Drawing Room

The hotel reopened on 29th November a few months later than the Royal Bath (4th September), despite being left in a mess with its furniture gone, carpets damaged and items having been stolen. The manger Ninian Wilson had successfully built up the Metropole and he was determined to restore the

Carlton's reputation. Marsham Court had headhunted Mr Wilson after the death of Mr Marsh but he accepted the Carlton's offer. He agreed however to help re-equip, refurbish, set up a management team and re-open The Marsham Court.

The Carlton had originally been built as a private house called Brumstath. In 1861 it was home to Nicholas Henry the Minister of Richmond Hill Congregational Church. Isabella Suffolk, niece to the Duke of Norfolk, was living there in 1871 and local Roman Catholics used it to celebrate mass. In May 1900 four businessmen, TJ Hankinson, GJ Lawson, JJ Allen and JE Beale, formed Bournemouth and District Property Company and they purchased the house with the idea of converting it into boarding houses. In the early days, Bournemouth targeted the professional classes who needed quality suites and wintered in the hotels with their own domestic staff. However the new shorter stays holiday market after the 1900s needed smaller rooms and used hotel staff. Suites were changed into bedrooms and a main dining room added. Neighbouring villas Broadly and Leeholme were added in 1909 and 1917 respectively. The Carlton also had the first electrically operated lift fitted in 1911.

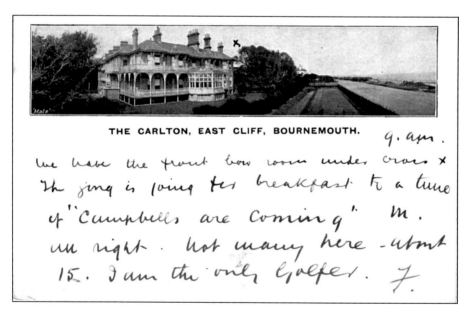

Carlton Hotel, 1905

Mrs Trigg was a formidable manager, from 1903-1913, on £150 p.a. plus 10% of the profits. She came from Thackeray's Hotel in London to the interview with the Directors of the Carlton before accepting the job. She ensured lights were turned out in the public rooms at 11 p.m. Meals were not served in bedrooms or sitting rooms or outside of stated times.

Breakfast was from 9-10 a.m. and for 2/- you could have rolls, toast, preserves, tea, coffee, cocoa or chocolate, porridge, fish and a variety of hot and cold dishes.

Luncheon was from 1-2 p.m. with soup, hot and cold joints, vegetables, sweets and cheese for 2/6d. If you wanted poultry it was 3/-.

Dinner was from 7-8 p.m. and for 5/- you could have soup, fish, entrees, joints, poultry or game, sweets and desserts. Visitors on inclusive terms needed to give notice on arrival and no allowance was made for non-attendance at meals. Baths were 1/- and fires in bedrooms and sitting rooms 1/6d or 2/- all day.

Carlton Hotel, 1940s

By March 1928, the Meyrick Estate granted The Carlton the right to call itself a hotel. Until then The Carlton was seen as a first-class residential establishment, handsomely furnished and appointed with daily or weekly rates from 4 guineas. The 1920s however had seen an economic decline and the running costs of the hotel were £118 per week. Staff were sacked including the Under Gardener on £2 13s 0d per week as being too expensive to maintain. By then the hotel was seen as mediocre although providing good food. By 1934 it had managed to achieve 5-star status and remained for many years the only privately owned 5-star hotel in Europe.

From 1918-1950s roadside posters advertising The Carlton were on all main routes into Bournemouth. The manager Mr Wilson also kept meticulous records of the visitors and produced several brochures for the different types of business including a brochure for passengers waiting to board the liners at Southampton.

In 1947 the hotel was granted a restaurant and residential licence, the first hotel on the East Cliff to obtain one. The restaurant was extended and bathrooms added to the bedrooms. By the 1950s it had an international reputation and was a favourite with Queen Elizabeth's great aunts Princess Helena Victoria and Princess Marie Louise.

In 1955 the Eden Suite was built for the Conservative conference with Sir Anthony Eden informing the hotel that he needed an extra bedroom for his wife. In those 36 hours it was achieved. In the 1960s it became part of a marketing group Prestige Hotels alongside the Lygon Arms (Broadway), Imperial Hotel (Torquay) and Whately Hall (Cotswolds).

The hotel "high on the bracing East Cliff" continued to attract top names from the sports world such as Bobby Moore, Rod Laver and Sir Matt Busby to politicians Harold MacMillan, Enoch Powell, 'Rab' Butler to entertainers Eartha Kitt, Morecambe and Wise and Sid James. The singer Andy Williams donated a lion cub 'Solitaire' after his hit record in 1973 to the hotel where it was sent to join the other lions at Longleat.

Field Marshall Montgomery (82 at the time), a favourite guest at the hotel, was invited to signal the pulling down of the East Wing. He gave the command to the bulldozer driver, a former Desert Rat, but the wall refused to fall and Montgomery remarked that he would have a word at Bovington to borrow some tanks. The new East Wing was 'topped out' in 1970 with a Methuselah of champagne and 49 bedrooms and two penthouses were built at a cost of £350,000. Guest could enjoy a colour television, fridge and lights that if you pressed for a few seconds would switch all the lights out so that you didn't have to leave your bed. One couple that didn't quite understand the system unscrewed all the light bulbs. The East Wing was later converted into timeshare apartments which lost the hotel 46% of its accommodation and its highest priced rooms.

In 1980 the hotel was sold to Frederick Losel who sold it to Peter Bailey in 1989 (owner of the nearby Miramar) only for both hotels to be put in the hands of the administrator in 1993. Since 1996 it has been part of the Menzies group.

Post-War Years

The 1946 guide sent out to prospective visitors was the 1939 guide with assurances that almost all pre-war entertainment was open and it hoped to: "recommence steamship pleasure sailings for summer 1946. The indoor bowling green, ice rink and Boscombe Pier are closed. Visitors should bring their ration books or obtain Emergency Card from local Food Office."

In July 1946, the murder of 21 year old Doreen Marshall by Neville Heath in Bournemouth hit the headlines. Heath had booked into the Tollard Royal Hotel under the name Group Captain Rupert Brooke. This was his downfall as Detective Suter was suspicious about Heath's scant knowledge of the RAF.

Heath took Miss Marshall out for dinner and after offering to walk her back to her hotel (Norfolk Hotel, Richmond Hill) brutally attacked and killed her. The police made enquiries at hotels and boarding houses but were hindered, as the description did not match Neville Heath. In his room (number 81) they found a blood stained scarf and a worn leather riding whip.

The Tollard Royal was owned by Mr Butterworth in 1924. It had a large ballroom and accommodation for 100 visitors and cost 15/6d per day. In 1956 it was converted to flats.

Tollard Royal Hotel, 1954

Bournemouth however found people were determined to have a holiday; despite the neglected state of the beach and a lack of pre-war entertainment, accommodation was in short supply. Hotels were also being sold especially to people who found it hard to settle back in their old jobs after the war. Typical was the family from Wales who in 1948 bought the small private hotel, The Brockenhurst at 66, St Michaels Road (now flats) for £7,500. There were fourteen bedrooms all with hot and cold water but only one bathroom and an extra toilet on the ground floor. The owners offered personal attention but no permanent residencies were allowed.

Meanwhile beach huts started to be put back, cliff railings and seats replaced. The pier was still missing its middle section and repairs would not begin until August 1947. In September 1946, a mine disturbed by rough seas exploded breaking windows in a Southbourne hotel and causing a cliff fall.

By 1948 hoteliers were complaining in their trade magazine that the bad winter season in 1947 was not helped by Bournemouth Corporation's lack of advertising. Although the Local Government Act allowed part of the rates to be used for advertising in the British Isles, Bournemouth's advertising was less than the pre-war level. The local hotel association accused the corporation of being ill-advised and grumbled about the lack of sufficient information and literature on forthcoming events to send to visitors.

They also despaired of hotels dropping their prices: "What can a hotelier give for 9/- a day, even in a place where the proprietor and his wife do all the work themselves? Remember that to cover expenditure on food, laundry and wages is not enough." The Hotel Association warned their members there is a "danger of Bournemouth getting a reputation for being a cheap jack town and in summer for charging exorbitant prices because the summer terms are nearly double the winter". (The *Daily Mirror* had described the hotel-keepers as being grasping as prices soared.)

The weather was inclement in August 1948 and visitor numbers were low with spending up in the shops but down on the steamers and motor tours. There had also been complaints from visitors about the lack of refreshments on the trains to Bournemouth from Lancashire and Yorkshire.

Some hoteliers had other problems. Mr Joseph Grower from the Rubens Hotel on November 23rd 1948 took a former guest (Mr Loebe) to court by claiming £72 as the guest left early after four days into his stay because he had heard that a child in the hotel had measles. Mr Grower lost the case with Judge Armstrong announcing it was the hotelkeeper's duty to inform parents and to limit the spread of infectious diseases. The Rubens Hotel (formerly called The Bourne) was later demolished and is now the site of a roundabout on Bath Road.

Bourne Hotel, 1930

On the 17th August Bournemouth Pier was re-opened. A temporary gangway linked the stumps and the buildings were rebuilt in 1950. Boscombe Pier wasn't re-opened until the 1960s.

Hotels everywhere faced a much-changed world. People were no longer booking for the winter months and day trips in coaches meant "full board" was giving way to "bed, breakfast and evening meal". Hotels had to adjust to a different type of customer. The wealthy that had visited during late autumn and winter were almost non-existent in the post-war period. Hotels now welcomed coach parties instead. It was said there were 2,000 places offering accommodation in the early 1950s, many of them small and only about 20-30 hotels were licensed.

With a depression hitting the hotel trade the hotels were still battling with the Council over expenditure on advertising, with the £10,000 allocation being the same as the previous year. Councillors retaliated saying more hoteliers should come forward to serve on the Council! This was emphasised again in 1951 where Councillors couldn't understand why the hotels objected to any sport on Sunday in Bournemouth, as surely their visitors would appreciate playing or watching sport.

One hotelier, Mr William Hackett from Towercliffe in Cliff Cottage Road obviously decided to take their advice and was a candidate for Winton but in 1960 failed to "transmit to the appropriate officer his election expenses".

Enquiries for the *Bournemouth Guide* were up in January 1950 but fell in February due to the General Election. Later that year the British Tourist Holiday Board brought out a report on its survey of hotels which had checked on the reception, service generally, attitudes of hotel staff, flexibility of meal times, dining room service, tipping, toilet facilities, licensing restrictions, comfort, amenities, bedroom accommodation, food (especially with regard to the 5/- limit).

The Mayor Sydney Thomson was obviously concerned when he wrote in the Hotel Association's Bulletin: "Most lasting impression is created whether for good or ill, by the hotel or boarding house at which the visitor stays. Prosperity of a resort such as our own can be materially affected by the attitude of those who cater for visitors."

Easter 1951 was the wettest for 11 years and the coldest for 14 years and followed a hard and expensive winter season. There were complaints about the disappearing sand from the beaches at Bournemouth, Boscombe and Southbourne.

The Beach at Whitsun, 1950s

However in the 1950s Bournemouth still boasted a million visitors a year. The town still resisted shops on the cliff top and only allowed municipal cafes on the Undercliff. The visitors in the South's premier resort could however go to a different entertainment every night including seven live shows.

The writer JRR Tolkien (Lord of the Rings fame) spent his holidays in the 1950s and 1960s at the Miramar Hotel, East Overcliff Drive, always staying in rooms 37 and 39. He wrote whilst his wife enjoyed the facilities of the hotel. In 1920 it had been called The Edgar Steel Hotel but from 1921-1936 it was the Hinton Court Private Jewish Pension. In 1938 it changed its name to Hotel Miramar and from the 1950s-1975 was run by Steel Hotels Ltd. In the 1969 guide Mr and Mrs Douglas Steel advertised the Miramar as being "An Hotel of Unusual Charm". With AA and RAC status it had a night porter and there were telephones in every room.

Miramar Hotel

The holiday guides for the 1950s were keen on quoting Thomas Hardy's description of Bournemouth: "A new world in an old one." They were however at pains to point out, "In speaking of Bournemouth as a modern town there is one impression we must not convey. It would be quite wrong to think of it as featuring promenades and thoroughfares with continuous facades of concrete. On the contrary its modernity is expressed by nature, which was the foundation for its success, to disappear, it has been quite effectively preserved." "Superlatives fall easily from the pen in describing Bournemouth."

Entertainment was numerous with four theatres, The Pavilion staging West End shows, ballet, opera, pantomime and a ballroom tea lounge. The New Royal put on summer shows, The Palace Court (now part of the Premier Inn, Westover Road) presented modern plays and the Hippodrome showed variety shows. The Winter Gardens were home to the Bournemouth Symphony Orchestra and shows featuring radio and television stars. In the summer, two forms of entertainment the Water Show featured were speciality and comedy diving, water turns and water ballet. The Ice Show took the form of a revue with exhibition and comedy skating with well-known ice skaters. Hotels, of course, also put on their own entertainment such as the jazz club in the basement of The Chines, 9 Rosemount Road where well-known artists such as Oscar Petersen and John Dankworth were said to have played.

The Chines Hotel, 1961

The guides warned prospective visitors that demands on accommodation were heavy during the busy season and encouraged people to visit in springtime, May and June having the most sunshine and least rain. Those people too "busily occupied in the summer also choose Bournemouth for a late holiday". "The Christmas and Easter Holidays are so popular that it is wise to make hotel reservations well in advance."

There were 25 licensed hotels (bars open to non residents) 290 unlicensed hotels and boarding houses and 165 bed and breakfast establishments advertising in the 1959 guide. The Carlton and Grand Hotel (Firvale Road) had 150 bedrooms each and the smallest hotel, run by Mrs Peckham in Capstone Road, let one room.

It may have been difficult for visitors to choose where to stay. Many of the hotels were extolling their modernity, interior sprung mattresses, liberal servings of varied food, hot and cold water in all rooms and spacious lounges. There are some advertisements, which catch your attention. One such advert in 1959 is for The Elstead where "Our Target is your Happiness" and "Test our H-Bomb of Happiness" and "Make Warfare on the Blues". This was a little different to their 1957 advert extolling their efficient central heating, Swiss chef and late night porter.

The Cotford Hall Hotel, 30-32 Knyveton Road boasted: "A place in the sun and a place for your son." Langdale Hotel, 6 Earle Road Alum Chine, promised: "A happy carefree holiday, comfortable and homely with no vexatious restrictions."

Toft House Hotel (East Overcliff Drive) used a quote from Elizabeth Nicolas (Travel Correspondent of the *Sunday Times*) to tempt visitors: "I am happy to record that the Toft House Hotel in which we spent the night was the best run Hotel it has been my fate to visit for a very long time."

The Toft House Hotel, 1939

Quinney's Hotel (12 Durley Road, West Cliff) boasted, "Perhaps there is an air of antiquity pervading, for here in fact Quinneys was written." (HA Vachell wrote several Quinney books about an antiques dealer.) Obviously they were not pursuing the modern route.

The 1950s did see complaints from overseas visitors on the state of British hotels, mainly the lack of private bathrooms, inadequate heating in bedrooms and poorly cooked food. Hoteliers moaned that the buildings were not easy to adapt and staff were in short supply and too expensive. Money to improve hotels was not forthcoming and the Government, even with MPs in constituents where hotels were important to the local economy, didn't understand tourism. Some hotels obviously did make improvements but many did not see any need to, especially with currency restrictions making holidaying abroad difficult. Even by 1966 when a survey was made of British hotels with private bathrooms, in 55 Bournemouth hotels only two had 100% en-suite rooms, five had 50%, eight had 25%, 27 had less than 25% and 13 had no en-suite rooms. From 48 resorts, only Torquay, Bournemouth, Brighton and Great Yarmouth had a hotel with 100% private bathrooms. In 1968, The Wessex Hotel had 95 bedrooms but only 17 had private bathrooms. The bedrooms did have radio, intercom and some had baby listening devices.

Quinney's Hotel, 1960

The local Bournemouth Hotel Association were urging members to consider their guests needs. "Check that all bells work properly and do they annoy guests by being too far away from an armchair or beds? In the cocktail bar are there enough seats for middle-aged people?" By 1953 arguments over the merits of putting televisions in lounges raged. Some saw it as an infliction on visitors who wanted to use the public lounge to read while others were saying that if we encourage people to stay in what happens to other entertainment?

Easter 1953 was busy in Bournemouth with many visitors coming on chance. The Hotel Association called for a clearing house "to be set up for hotels with last minute vacancies". Hotels then found bookings down for the two weeks of the Coronation and costs rising (up by 9% on 1952 without including meat rationing); they asked the town for more advertising and better amenities. It can be seen throughout the fifties that prices were continuing to rise as electricity, gas and water prices were published in the holiday guides. Despite paper rationing after the war, the hoteliers demanded new editions of the *Bournemouth Guide* every year ready for distribution by 1st January. In 1953 80,000 copies were printed with an extra 20,000 for any alterations for the autumn. There was boost to pre-Christmas trade that year when a dense fog on

5-8th December diverted London bound planes to Hurn airport bringing business to many hotels from stranded passengers.

Visitors, as now, continued to be a source of stories with Mr Norris of Red Roofs Hotel (formerly The Grosvenor and now part of the Belvedere) being upset by the number of visitors who came to Reception to 'borrow' ink for their fountain pens. He put a card out giving the address of the nearest post office! Another landlady had rented a room to two men she did not know and was a little worried. However after a few days she explained to other hoteliers she had stopped fretting. "They must be nice boys. They have towels from the Y.M.C.A."

The Times in July 1955 ran a feature on Bournemouth "this prosperous resort" naming it: "a Queen among Britain's shopping centres". It seemed shopping was a "holiday adventure" enjoyed by women and "patiently endured" by men. Business for the shops was better than Christmas in July and August when the town was full of visitors from the North and Midlands.

Jennifers, 1960

Hotels such as Jennifers in West Hill Road previously a domestic residence called Fieldenstein) advertised Saturday to Saturday bookings only during the summer season. No reductions were made for temporary absence! For a small hotel it was a long day for proprietors starting with early morning tea trays,

102

breakfast, lunch, tea (at 4 p.m.), dinner and late evening refreshments. It was no surprise that if guests wanted meals in their rooms, there was an extra charge.

By 1958 the local Hotel Association celebrated their silver jubilee. It had been formed to bring hoteliers together to work for better trading conditions and better standards. In the ensuing twenty-five years there had been a considerable change in social conditions including holidays with pay. This had increased the number of people taking holidays, including taking holidays abroad.

Local MP John Eden wrote: "These 25 years have not been easy, scarred by the war, beset with administration problems, beleaguered by high taxes and heavy costs, your industry has certainly had its full share of the difficulties which have faced us all."

One hotelier was asked by a visitor if he had been away as he was quite tanned. His answer was no, but his kitchen sink faced south! His business was like many other boarding houses/hotels at that time. It was the era of people booking the same hotel, the same room and the same week or weeks from year to year. It was guaranteed business from Easter to October but it wasn't to last much longer.

Bournemouth Square, 1956

Jewish Hotels

Bournemouth had several Jewish hotels and from the 1940s until the end of 1970s they were often the epitome of luxury. Many offered all-inclusive holidays with entertainment, full board and swimming pools. The top Jewish hotel was undoubtedly Green Park (formerly Keverstone Court Hotel) in Manor Road (now flats) owned by the Marriott and Richman families. They had moved from Torquay in 1943 having bought the modern (built 1936) luxury 59-bed hotel. It was one of the first to have a bathroom in every bedroom. Operating as an Orthodox Jewish hotel it attracted very wealthy clientele. The all-inclusive hotel had a children's TV room, playground, children's swimming pool as well as another pool, tennis courts, dancing entertainment and its own synagogue. It was constantly being refurbished and upgraded to keep up with the demands of its guests. Staff were brought in from Italy where their hotel schools ensured good waiting staff. The Jewish New Year would bring in youngsters at the end of the Italian summer season with many of them opting to stay and work in the hotel for many years.

Green Park Hotel, 1947

Another Jewish hotel in Bournemouth was the Majestic in Derby Road run by Fay Shnyder (now owned by Shearings Coaches.) In 1876 it had been Saugeen Primary School, where John Galsworthy the writer of the Forsyth

Saga had been a pupil. In August 1935 the hotel had a foundation stone ceremony to mark its rebuilding.

However by the 1960s with kosher hotels opening in Israel and the limit on the amount of money allowed out of Britain lifted, guests still came to the Green Park and other Jewish hotels but shortened their stays from six weeks or more to about two weeks. In the 1970s with the market still changing, the Green Park introduced package holidays and a very popular golf tournament in November. Mr Marriott experienced ill health in the 1980s and the hotel was sold in 1986 to the owner of East Cliff Manor and the Majestic (a non Jewish hotel by then) to be run as his flagship hotel. It was then sold to developers, demolished and flats built in 1993.

MAJESTIC HOTEL • BOURNEMOUTH •

The Majestic Hotel in the 1960s

The Cumberland on East Overcliff Drive was a Jewish hotel run by the Felds (The Cumberland had been opened in 1949). In 1973 the hotel offered personal service, entertainment and had 105 bedrooms with radio. It had its own Synagogue and was possibly the largest Orthodox Jewish hotel in Europe. The hotel was sold in 1984 to Eric Wright, part owner of the Majestic, being again sold in 1988 to the Young Hotel group.

Other Jewish Hotels included The Ambassador in Meyrick Road (now the Britannia) and The Langham in Meyrick Road. In 1931 it was non Jewish and run by Mr and Mrs W Mayger. It had five reception rooms, forty-two bedrooms with central heating throughout and a beach hut for bathing. (It is now the Queens and was once part of the Young Hotel Group. In 1988 the Queens had twenty-two choices for starters on the lunch menu and a thought of the day.)

Langham Hotel, 1940s

In his book *Secrets, Boyhood in a Jewish hotel 1932-54* Ronald Hayman writes of growing up in his Granny's East Cliff Court Hotel (East Overcliff Drive and now part of the Menzies group.) He recalls inverted rowing boats on the beach with the fishing nets drying and fish being landed. He remembers buying bananas and oranges on the beach and watching the Bird Lady feeding the birds by the bandstand in the pleasure gardens.

Langham Hotel, 1930

Ronald Hayman loved Christmas at the hotel where on Christmas Eve the guests were given a present from Granny as they came into the dining room, usually a little leather diary with East Cliff Court Bournemouth in silver print on the front. There would be a Christmas party for the children in the cocktail lounge with crackers and paper hats, cabaret and dancing every night in the ballroom until New Year. As a child growing up in a hotel it meant the visitors were the most important people so making too much noise or running in the corridor was not allowed.

The East Cliff and Sands, 1910

Southbourne Beach, 1920

It also meant he never had to clean his shoes, cook or wash up! In 1939 the RAF wanted to requisition the hotel and the family moved into a rented house. Moving out of the hotel upset his grandmother as she thought nothing would be the same again. She was right, there had only been one other Jewish hotel in the town before the war and now there were others, including a serious rival that had opened during the war offering free cocktails and cabarets with top Jewish comedians.

Children's Corner, Pleasure Gardens, 1920s

The Normandie in Manor Road was another large Jewish hotel. It was just a private house in 1872 and from 1885-1916 the home of several consecutive doctors before becoming Hotel Normandie in 1937. The hotels had loyal customers who booked every year, as Bournemouth was the Jewish family holiday destination. The hotels all vied for business and The Normandie was especially well known for its lavish kiddushes on Shabbat. It was also perceived as more religious and many of the more strictly observant Jews stayed here. It had its own on-site ministers and was seen as a safe place for children with its two acres of garden. The Normandie also provided separate entertainment for men and women.

It was however the last kosher hotel to survive as the Jewish hotels, like other hotels in the town, suffered as visitors took holidays aboard. Plans to demolish the hotel and build four maisonettes and 38 flats were turned down in 2005. Plans for holiday flats were also refused in 2007 but planning was granted for 43 holiday flats and 10 residential flats in 2008. Now there is nowhere in Bournemouth providing kosher food. Former synagogues in hotels such as at the New Ambassador are now conference rooms.

Normandie Hotel, 1970s

Boscombe

In the 1860s Boscombe was basically the Shelley estate and a few cottages. However by 1865 developers moved in with two very different schemes. Boscombe Spa with its marine villas was from Sea Road to Boscombe Chine (land allocated to the Earl of Malmesbury in 1805). North of the main road, Palmerston, Shelley and Ashley Roads were sites for smaller artisan houses and some shops. Properties fronting the Christchurch Road had to be detached or semi detached dwelling houses bound by small white brick walls.

In 1872, the Boscombe Spa Hotel Company was formed with plans to build a first class hotel, with its own pleasure grounds and a winter garden. Keen to be part of the fashion for taking the waters, the company decided to open up a temporary hotel in 1873. Natural springs of mineral waters had been discovered at the bottom of the chine and Sir Henry Wolff had a thatched summerhouse built over the spot. Former Foreign Office Diplomat (British Minister at Madrid and MP for Christchurch) Sir Henry Drummond Wolff had a seaside house, Boscombe Towers near to where the Burlington Hotel would later be built.

Boscombe Chine, 1905

The Boscombe Spa hotel was opened in September 1874 with suites, smoking room and a coffee room with views over the Channel and the Isle of Wight. Wolff quoted a Temple Bar writer, "Sitting on the terrace of the Chine Hotel, sheltered from the East Wind and gazing over the sandhills of the deep blue and almost tideless sea I can fancy that I am on the southern shores of the Mediterranean. A distinguished artist said that it required only the presence of some camels standing about for him to imagine himself in Africa." Expensive to build it was seen as one of the most attractive hotels in the south with its Elizabethan style half timbers. However by April 1880 the hotel closed and the contents auctioned. The building was taken over by Bournemouth College and the school ran for the next five years. By 1888 the building had been enlarged and was once again a hotel, the Boscombe Chine Hotel. In *Brights Illustrated Guide to Bournemouth 1888* it was described as having: "the finest position on the famed East Cliff. The house has been much enlarged, redecorated and beautifully furnished throughout by eminent London firms and the sanitary arrangements are perfect as has been testified by the Medical Officer of Health and Local Sanitary Authorities." Thomas Phillips was the proprietor and Miss Williams the Manageress.

Boscombe Chine Hotel, 1908

The Chine Hotel requested their visitors, in the early part of the 20th century, "to enter their names in the arrival book to facilitate the delivery of letters". The hotel offered excellent stabling at Chine Mews although a horse omnibus met trains by arrangement. If visitors wanted a bath they could have a sponge or hip bath for 6d and in the bathroom it was 1/- for a cold bath and 1/6d for a hot bath. By 1950 it was run by the Butterworths, a Bournemouth hotel family who still own a number of hotels in the area. With the hotel's connection with the Opera House and other theatres they urged visitors to stay at "Bournemouth's leading holiday hotel. Stay with the leading stars of radio and stage. Bargain holiday terms."

Boscombe Beach, 1953

In 2009 after a refurbishment, a new bar and brasserie was opened on the theatrical theme celebrating the hotel's famous guests including Laurel and Hardy, Norman Wisdom, Harry Secombe and Peter Sellers.

Boscombe was developing as a seaside resort and calls were being made in 1884 for the building of a pier. The Bournemouth Improvement Commissioners refused to finance the £8,000 scheme and it was left to local entrepreneurs. The Boscombe Pier Company applied to the Board of Trade for an order to build a pier. One of their directors was Mr T Phillips of the Boscombe Chine Hotel. A gala celebration of the first pile being driven on the 17th October 1888 ended in a public lunch at the hotel.

During the late 1890s Boscombe was growing rapidly and the two separate sections had merged. Although now officially part of the borough of Bournemouth it retained its own identity. There were a number of hotels and boarding houses and it had its own railway station in 1885.

Advertised as: "Cool in summer, warm in winter" Boscombe claimed to be "the healthiest health resort in all the land."

Boscombe Chine, early 1900s

Boscombe Gardens, 1910

In 1890 Mr Archibald Beckett (a developer) began his extensive building operations including a first class hotel The Salisbury. It was an imposing site alongside the all-weather attraction, The Royal Arcade. According to *An*

Illustrated Guide to Bournemouth 1893, the public entrance was in Palmerston Road and the private and hotel entrance in Christchurch Road, through "a spacious tile paved hall, on the right and left of which run lofty corridors to the various apartments." The dining room had a lift "communicating with the kitchens, so that the food is served hot from the ovens." There were several suites, a large bathroom with hot and cold baths and about fifty bedrooms. The "drawing room is on the first floor, and is approached by a handsome broad staircase, thickly carpeted."

The local covenant of private residences had been lifted allowing this area to be used for shops and entertainment. In the *Bournemouth Guide* for 1911 it boasted sitting "on highest point of the Borough the position is bracing and invigorating." It was also the "only residential licensed hotel on Christchurch Road." It had an "Electrophone in connection with the Winter Gardens Band." This was a system where headphones were hired and connected through Bayley's exchange to microphones at the Winter Gardens. The proprietor WJ McCabe offered en pension from 7/6d per day with special terms for visitors making a long stay. The Salisbury Hotel was built on the site of a villa and is today where McDonalds and Greens Pub are situated.

Salisbury Hotel, 1927

Further down the Christchurch Road, Mr Exton opened the Linden Hall Boarding Establishment in 1890 on the corner of Knole Road and opposite Chine Gardens. (From 1884 the upper parts of the gardens were leased and the brickfield site became lawn and tennis courts.)

Boscombe Gardens, early 1907

Mr Exton extended his 10-bed roomed house (Linden Vale) and after successive extensions from 1893-1903 the Linden Hall had 100 bedrooms. After his death, his son Leo Exton took over running the hotel in 1918. It became the Linden Hall Hydro in 1934 when a swimming and sports stadium was added at a cost of £10,000.

By 1939 it was part of a group of hotels which included The Burlington, Sandbanks Hotel, Grosvenor and Royal Victoria Hotels at Swanage. It had 120 bedrooms, a garage for 70 cars and all rooms had gas or electric fires. In the sports and swimming stadium there were all manner of medical treatments including Studa Chair, diarthermy, faradism and Turkish, Russian and Hydro baths. The hotel employed a Lady Hostess whose job it was to arrange the daily amusements.

Like many hotels handed back after the war, the Linden Hall had suffered. The flat roof had been used for exercise and the damage caused allowed rain to pour in. Some of the rooms had been used by the Americans to lock up offenders and the banisters and skirting ripped up and used for fuel. There was no furniture and the owner only received £15,000 in compensation.

115

Linden Hall Hydro, 1930s

By 1956 The Linden Hall Hydro welcomed families to Bournemouth's all-seasons hotel with prices in June from 10 guineas. If not content with the activities in the hotel, children could paddle in the small pond in the gardens or ride on a pony stabled at the end of the chine. Along the seafront there was the Peter Pan miniature railway and parents were safe in the knowledge the Undercliff was only open to pedestrians in the summer until dusk. At night the gardens in Bournemouth and Boscombe were illuminated with fairy lights.

By 1968 the hotel had dropped the name Hydro and was simply Linden Hall Hotel advertising its famous swimming pool. The Exton family left the hotel in 1973. By 1974 there were fewer rooms as private bathrooms were becoming more popular. Central heating and phones and radios were to be found in the rooms. Sport was still encouraged and included judo, karate and fencing.

The *1982 Bournemouth Guide* shows the hotel under the resident managers Susan and Laurence Belcher, the "Hotel with the personal touch" had lost its sports and swimming pool to the Lanz Hotel group with The Lanz Sportz centre opening in 1980 behind the hotel in Knole Road. It offered squash, saunas, billiards, yoga, licensed restaurant and ample parking. The hotel offered full board at £66-£99 plus VAT and even took American Express and Diners cards. It had been put up for sale in 1978 but finally closed in 1983.

By 1985 it had been demolished. Susan Belcher was quoted as saying, "I am absolutely heartbroken to see the hotel coming down." And thus 72-78 Christchurch Road became Linden Hall flats. The sports centre continued as a

David Lloyd Centre until its owners Whitbreads sold it for development in 2007.

Boscombe Chine Gardens, 1900s

On 20th October 1892 the "charmingly placed" freehold of Boscombe Towers and Tankerville were sold by the Meyrick Estate to a syndicate who wanted to build a large grand hotel. The builder Mr Chappell won the tender to build the Burlington Hotel for £23,000. It however eventually probably cost more than £70,000. It boasted 200 bedrooms, 13 suites, and a ballroom and was opened in August 1893 with a lunch and garden party. In *Brights Guide to Bournemouth 1895* it was advertised as a: "Country mansion, perfectly unique, practically designed, sumptuously furnished and fitted throughout."

From 11th July-16th July 1910 the hotel was booked for the participants in the Bournemouth Aviation Meeting famously remembered for the death of the Hon CS Rolls when his Wright bi-plane broke up and crashed. The 1939 guide shows it as supplying sea water to bathrooms, having a modern cocktail lounge and standing in its own spacious grounds complete with three tennis courts.

The Burlington had been requisitioned during the war and it never recovered as a hotel. In 1948 plans were passed for it to become flats but it continued as a hotel when it was bought for £79,000 in 1950. It closed in 1955 with plans for flats being erected on the site but this was refused in 1957. However in 1960 plans for 352 flats were granted but the hotel failed to reach its reserve price. On 12th January 1962 it opened the first casino club in

Bournemouth. It continued to struggle and there were plans to convert it into an old people's home. 1964 saw another plan for it to become a shopping precinct turned down and the Burton family bought it for £175,000 in 1972. In 1976 it became a Grade II listed building and was sold to a Bournemouth business group in 1984 for £800,000. It is now flats.

2503   HOTEL BURLINGTON, BOSCOMBE.
                          TELEPHONE: BOSCOMBE 58.

Burlington Hotel, 1920s

Other large hotels in Boscombe included the Tarrazona on the corner of Christchurch Road and Crabton Close Road. In 1927 they used "all farm produce from Devonshire" and "Best English Meat only". It is now shops and flats. The Fircroft in Owls Road in 1928 had "full size tennis and croquet courts, bathing tent, First-Class Orchestra, winter games and Instructor gives lessons daily in all modern dances". The hotel was demolished in 2009 for residential development.

Boscombe had mainly smaller boarding and guesthouses. In April 1892 plots in the Boscombe Spa Estate were sold for development, including 12 sites in Georgiana Road (now St. John's Road) that were suitable for nice comfortable little villas instead of large boarding houses. It wasn't long before the majority became guesthouses including No. 4 Firscot (now Minton Lodge), No. 8 Bathwick Lodge Guest House, No. 10 Golden Sands, No. 21 Dunvegan, No. 23 Holmleigh, Belfield Hotel. In 1957 Conway Court, 6 St John's Road (now The Rosscourt) offered "Gas fires and Bedside lights, Interior Sprung

118

Mattresses" for 5-6 guineas. Originally the home of T Annen (bootmaker) in 1904 it became 'Fuji-Yama' and the home of the Andrews family from 1914 to the 1940s.

Fircroft Hotel, 1930

Rosscourt Hotel, 1968

Through the early and mid 20th century Boscombe prospered alongside her bigger neighbour Bournemouth. The sandy beach and safe bathing brought families either by car, coach or by train to Boscombe's own station, which was closed in 1965.

Boscombe Beach, 1920s

Guest houses and other hotels in Percy Road and Owls Road (named after a magazine *The Owl* founded by Boscombe resident Sir Algernon Borthwick) such as Sorrento, Gunreda, Knightlow, Boscombe Grange and Bramcote Hall have all disappeared.

Hotel Sorrento, 1983

Knightlow Hotel, 1950s

The recession and bad press given to the area in the 1980s and 1990s made trading difficult for the hoteliers and many sold out to developers. All the major hotels including The Courtlands have gone leaving The Chine the biggest hotel in the area.

Courtlands Hotel, 1930

The Chine Hotel, Boscombe

However in recent years after a long struggle Boscombe has benefited from a variety of grants and the Boscombe Chine Gardens were restored in 2007. In 2009 the Northern Hemisphere's first artificial surf reef was completed and opened 250 yards off Boscombe seafront. The Honeycombe Chine flats development (built on an old boating pond) has paid for the pier to be made safe and the entrance that was recently listed made more inviting as well as other seafront regeneration schemes.

Honeycombe Chine Flats, Boscombe

1960s

By the 1960s seaside resorts were beginning to feel the effect of car ownership. Whereas railways had brought visitors for their one or two week holiday, the car meant more freedom. Instead of staying by the sea, the car owner could stay inland at the ever-increasing number of caravan and campsites and visit the beach for the day. The British holiday had become a touring one with many visitors not booking a hotel but staying in a bed and breakfast establishment.

Boscobel Hall

The Devonshire Hotel

Hotels on Terrace Mount where no parking was available such as Tregonwell Towers, Boscobel Hall, Hotel Mount Royal and Studleigh Royal Hotel were particularly affected. They were compulsory purchased and bulldozed down to make way for a town centre car park.

The Devonshire Hotel on Richmond Hill was demolished in 1965 to make way for the Portman Building Society office (now the Nationwide).

In 1961 Bournemouth advertised itself as: "Britain's Loveliest Resort" and was regarded as the "product of a new age". By 1964 it was: "A well run and organised community" with "excellent entertainment facilities of all kinds, first class sporting and recreational opportunities, a shopping centre with stores to rival London. Hotels and boarding houses are most important to the visitor and Bournemouth is fortunate in having a very wide choice to suit all pockets, all anxious to play their part in providing for your comfort."

Bournemouth Looking West
Showing hotels on Bath Road in 1951 which were later bulldozed down.
The area is now the site of a car park.

Southern Hay, 1960

The cuts in the railway network by Dr Beeching resulted in the railway branch line from Bath and Salisbury, that terminated at Bournemouth West Station (next to Queen's Hotel, Westbourne), closing on 3rd October 1965.

Over the years the Pines Express train had brought thousands of holidaymakers from Birmingham and Manchester to Bournemouth including in 1950 a group of school children from Lancashire. They stayed for a week at the Southern Hay Hotel in Cambridge Road, costing their parents a total of £3 15s 0d including the train fare. Once in Bournemouth they took trips out to Lulworth, Wareham and Salisbury. The hotel run by Mr and Mrs Doble had its own 9-hole putting green, dancing and sports room with table tennis and darts.

With the closure of the station, hotels close by suffered. Bourne Hall, which had been Dr Philpot's private residence, in 1880 was a home for "not absolute invalids". Rooms facing north were not recommended except to those in robust health. Later it became a very successful hotel, run by the Gwynne family and it was where many of the social events were held by the local Hotel Association. By 1973 a new 5-star hotel was planned for the site with a ballroom, theatre and conference facilities but it was developed as flats for the elderly in 1987 instead. The name moved to another hotel (West Cliff Hall) on Priory Road.

Bourne Hall Hotel, 1930

Holdenhurst Road and other roads near to Bournemouth Central Station were full of small bed and breakfast establishments serving optional evening meals. In the 1950s they would have their regular guests who would be expected to go out during the day and not return until a stipulated time in the afternoon even if it was raining. It was popular for families to go down to the beach such as at Branksome Chine and where they might have had their photograph taken, picking it up the next day.

In 1968 British Rail (Southern Region) were keen to attract business back. They advertised their fast intercity service as: "The sane way to travel" urging potential visitors to visit Bournemouth: "You can send your luggage on in advance. Your favourite seat can be reserved on almost all trains from certain stations from 3/-. Light refreshments can be obtained and packed meals bought from station refreshment room. No fuss, no bother, no traffic jams to cope with."

The extra cars coming into the resort kept businesses going for another decade until major road plans such as the building of the Wessex Way (A338) shifted all the cars from what had been the main road into the town from the East. Dual carriageways, roundabouts and office blocks were built over compulsory purchased houses, guesthouses and hotels such as those on Lansdowne, Christchurch and St Swithun's Road.

Cavendish Hotel, 8 Christchurch Road, 1930

The spur road gave the town direct access from Ringwood instead of diversions through Boscombe or Winton. The Lansdowne Road had been a popular route into town and had many hotels and guesthouses. These included No. 49 Kelvedon Guest House, No. 51 Sherwood Grange Hotel, No. 52 Highbury, No. 58 Perran Court, No. 63 Kingswood Private Hotel, No. 64 Golden Acres Hotel, No. 66 Moorings Hotel and No. 81 Pine Ridge. Now the Wessex Way either runs through where they had been or has cut them off from the rest of the town.

Sherwood Grange, 1971

Pine Ridge, 1969

Guesthouses and hotels close to Bournemouth Central Station also felt the effects of car ownership. Being close to the station was once a selling point but this no longer applied. Southcote Road had many small guesthouses including No. 10 Lynden, No. 18 Bryric House and No. 14 Pendene Guest House. Knyveton Road "One of Bournemouth's finest tree lined avenues" had dozens of large establishments: Penrhyn Hotel (now flats), Dalbury Court Hotel, Cleeve Court, Knyveton Hall Hotel (now residential), No. 18 Pinelands Private

Hotel (now flats), No. 19 Linkfield Court (now a residential care home), No. 21, Woodheath (now flats), Derby Hall Hotel, No. 31 Kelvin Court "a children's paradise".

Knyveton Hall, 1930

The family who also ran the ice rink in Westover Road owned it. In 1961 Kelvin Court advertised, "Generous hospitality extended to all. Coal fires in lounges." "Breakfast 9am, Lunch 1pm, Tea 4pm, Dinner 6.30, Tea and biscuits 10.30." It is now part of the Carrington (formerly the Moat House). The receivers took over the hotel in 1976 and ran it as the Moat House. In 1986 the Queen's Moat group bought the 60-bed hotel (it originally had 12 bedrooms) and joined it with its new 39-bed hotel, The Moat House Hotel. It is now The Carrington Hotel and part of the Forestdale group.

Kelvin Court, 1959

Knole Hall was urging visitors to their "Well appointed hotel of character, ideally situated. Newly decorated and close fitted carpets throughout. Ample toilets and bathrooms" in 1968. Cotford Hall, 30-32 Knyveton Road, advertised in 1971: "Do you feel the call of Cotford Hall? Then get cracking with the packing." The hotel lasted a few more years before being demolished and the Kings Courtyard flats built.

Cotford Hall

The only other surviving large hotel in Knyveton Road is The Elstead, which was a lot smaller in 1928 when they advertised: "Individual attention to delicate visitors. Liberal fare daintily served. Homegrown vegetables and poultry. Congenial society."

Elstead Hotel, 1950s

Wimbledon Hall Hotel, 1930

Wimbledon Hall Hotel in Knyveton Road closed in October 1973 with the owners Mr and Mrs Harvey Blowfield stating they "would rather retire than let the 80 bed establishment pass out of family hands". It had been bought by Mr Horspool (Mrs Blowfield's father) in 1935 as a 35-bed hotel. Guests they remembered included a young child who had jumped out of a second floor window onto the tarmac below but luckily was not badly hurt. They also recalled the two 80-year old ladies who started to fight in the garage!

Wimbledon Hall Hotel, 1973

Treetops Hotel, 1969

Christchurch Road also had numerous hotels, many of which became holiday flats, then changing to residential flats. These included Chinepines (now Edward Court flats), Merton, 54 Christchurch Road (converted to flats) and Belgravia, 56 Christchurch Road which traded until the early 1990s. In 1971 Mr and Mrs Hall invited "you to bring your family" and "they welcome children, they expect to find some sand in the bedrooms". No. 44 Bourne Pines Hotel and No. 46 Lund Hotel were demolished for redevelopment. Treetops Hotel was demolished and a nursing home built in the 1990s.

Lynton Court, 1930

The new road system brought in office development along roads at the Lansdowne. Plans to turn Gervis Road into a dual carriageway were stopped and a large roundabout (St Swithun's) was built. Griffs Hotel on the corner of Gervis Road and Christchurch Road became offices for Bournemouth Church Housing Association later.

Balincourt, 1940s

Balincourt, 2000s

Other smaller hotels continue to trade including Lynton Court and The Balincourt, opposite at 58 Christchurch Road. In 1890 it was called Colebrook Grange and in 1903 was the home of Mr and Mrs Willey. By 1939 it was Balincourt Boarding House (named after Chateau Balincourt near Paris) and by 1974 it was a "Private Hotel, superior and homely" with dinner, bed and breakfast only in June, July and August with full board offered in the other months. By 1986 rooms were advertised with en-suite and their own colour TVs. Now it is a 5-star guest accommodation with individually designed rooms, making the most of the building's original Victorian features as well as offering modern facilities such as Wi-fi.

Imperial Hotel, 1907

By the 1960s hotels were expected to look modern and offer better facilities. Southcombe, No. 40 Christchurch Road (The Water Garden Hotel) was offering a "Home from Home" in 1968. "Family and commercial hotel selected for motorists." It later became the Britannia and with an extra storey, mansard roof and new front the original Victorian building was hidden. Few new hotels were built apart from The Roundhouse (opened April 1969). It was built on the site of the Imperial, which had closed a few years earlier, at the Lansdowne.

The Roundhouse was the first major hotel built in the town since 1938 and its cylindrical shape was seen as being very adventurous for Bournemouth. The pebble dashed concrete exterior and honeycombed car park was viewed as

133

sophisticated modernity and aimed at the business market. In the basement was The Cave Bar, a themed cheese and wine bar, providing "adventure and intrigue". Apparently it had quite a dubious reputation in the 1970's!! Televisions could be hired for 5/- per day or 30/- per week as TV lounges were still the norm for most hotels.

Roundhouse Hotel, 1981

The conference trade had been seen as a route for the town to take for a number of years. Resorts in Britain were being abandoned for places such as Spain with promises of guaranteed sunshine. In October 1960 *The Times* ran a story on the decline of Bournemouth as a hotel centre. Plans were however turned down to build an 18-storey (200ft high) hotel with conference hall on the site of the Royal Exeter Hotel citing excessive use of the site.

The 1960s saw hotels being built in Britain but there was no confidence in building at the seaside. The views often held were that hotels were for foreigners to run or managers were just retired officers or waiters. Some hoteliers in Bournemouth took the opportunity to sell up to developers and many hotels were demolished in the 1960s and 1970s. This can be seen by all the high rise flats which bear the name of hotels that stood on those sites such as Sandykeld, Hinton Wood, Roslin Hall, Solent Pines and Crag Head. The original Crag Head built in 1870 had in 1881 been a royal residence for King Oscar II of Norway and Sweden.

Sandykeld, 1939

In 1965 a scheme was approved for a £4 million development on the seafront including Boscombe Pier and Honeycombe Chine. It was to include a 6-storey high hotel, multi-storey car park for 1,000 cars, conference hall, a casino, Olympic swimming pool, skyline restaurant, hostel for foreign students, shops and a night club.

By 1971, a £53 million plan was announced to attract US business. Not all were convinced, however, that the plan was viable. Some doubted anything spent over £5 million would see any return on the money. It was quoted as Bournemouth having over 800 hotels and boarding houses with the annual tourist revenue being £25 million, the town was seen as being too small and the scheme too reliant on US business men, their wives and fringe elements of conventions for it to work.

In June 1973 the *Caterer and Hotelkeeper* ran an article on Bournemouth and its loss of hotels. They stated 2,000 rooms had been lost over the previous 5 years as hotels were redeveloped as flats. It was more profitable for hoteliers to sell up than stay open. Back in December 1968 the Council had introduced a zoning policy to prevent any development that was seen as detrimental to the hotel industry especially on the East and West Cliffs. However by 1973 the zone was to be expanded. The Director of Tourism Joe Finn said, "I am particularly alarmed when I see big hotels like the Majestic disappearing. It is a matter of great concern that a unique Jewish hotel should close – particularly as Bournemouth is famous throughout Europe for its Jewish hotels on the East Cliff." The Majestic was on a list due for demolition in June 1973 after having been bought by a development company wanting to build 6 two-storey flats. It was however sold on behalf of Metropolitan Estates who also owned the Avon Royal and Beverley Hall Hotels (both empty) and after a £150,000 refit was reopened in May 1976.

Avon Royal, 1960

The Avon Royal on Christchurch Road was reputed to have been visited by royalty in Victorian times. It was sold in November 1978 and Mr Baxter who owned the Hazelwood next door spent £10,000 bringing the derelict hotel up to date. Both hotels were later demolished to build the Travelodge.

The Hazelwood Hotel

Durley Hall, 1927

Other hotels including the elite Green Park Hotel had their planning application for flats deferred whilst the Norfolk Royal applied to be redeveloped as offices. The Suncliff had its planning application for flats rejected and to save the Durley Hall Hotel on the West Cliff, the Council bought it for £280,000 so it could be leased out. In 1904 Durley Hall had been a boarding establishment run by a Mr Manwaring. In 1922 the owners Mr F Walker (Bournemouth) Ltd. offered croquet, clock golf and billiards for three guineas per week in his "Select Board Residence".

Durley Hall Hotel (now called Hallmark)

In 1923 well-known hoteliers the Burrs were in charge having redecorated and refurbished it until it was requisitioned in 1939. It was a training establishment for important personnel who managed Winfrith Atomic Energy. They only moved out in the 1960s to their new headquarters leaving the hotel derelict until the early 1970s. It had just one bedroom with its own bathroom! On August 1st 1997 the hotel was robbed by a masked gunman who took £10,000. The manger Jon Shipp sent the terrified staff home.

The 1970s saw the compulsory purchase by the Council of Westminster Hall, Meyrick Cliffs and Solent Cliffs in Beacon Road, and Regent Palace (built on the site of Darwin's Cliff Cottage) and Beechcliffe Hall both in Cliff Cottage Road.

Solent Cliffs Hotel 1931

The Council had over the years submitted several plans including a £16 million scheme to develop a tourist and conference centre including a 500-bed hotel in 1972. The Conference trade was doing well with numbers of conferences booked in 1974, up on 1973, to 220. The head of tourism reported that delegate spend was twice that of holidaymakers. The corner of Priory Road and Exeter Road had also seen alterations. The Sunnyside Hotel had been used as an annex to the Priory Hotel in 1897. Later it was called Cranborne Lodge then Exeter Court and let out as flats. In 1935 plans were submitted and refused for flats and shops; the following year plans for a 100-bed hotel were also refused. By 1946 a scheme for a coach station was shelved when the widening of Exeter Road took land from the hotel site making the property unsafe. It was demolished and in 1955 became a car showroom and offices and is now Keystone House.

The appetite for a seaside holiday at this time did not diminish; it merely transferred itself to newer and more attractive resorts abroad. Spain now settled after the civil war years became a cheap alternative to many British resorts. New purpose-built hotels, sunshine and cheap flights lured British holidaymakers away.

A survey by Metzner revealed in 1975 Bournemouth had 80,000 bed spaces with only half of the five million visitors totally satisfied, citing problems with traffic and parking. 64% of the visitors chose the same type of accommodation each year and preferred to stay in the centre of Bournemouth. The favoured activity was going to the beach, followed by shopping and sightseeing. Most people stayed on average seven days and brought £100 million to the local economy.

With national reluctance of tourism bodies to promote the seaside in favour of more traditional English places such as Oxford, Stratford upon Avon and The Lake District, it was left to the resorts themselves to fight for survival. In 1979 the local Hotel Association wrote of their concerns not of the conference trade but the disturbing sign of a fundamental decline over the traditional summer trade. They wanted a decision on the West Cliff site declaring a new conference and leisure centre would give the town a new lease of life. They wanted it to have an aspect of leisure, with universal marketing appeal such as the Eiffel Tower, for it to be economically viable and not to be concerned with conference or exhibition trade.

West Cliff Beach
West Cliff Sands showing the hotels that were demolished for the BIC site.

1980s - 1990s

By 1980 the Council were committed to building a conference and leisure centre. There were other rivals for the conference trade such as Harrogate and Brighton but Bournemouth had a good supply of hotels with star ratings. It had taken eight years, cost £2½ million but at last a six-acre site had been acquired to build the Bournemouth International Centre (BIC). During the compulsory purchase the hotels were leased on one-year leases. In February 1981 five hotels were pulled down including the site of the former Empress Hotel, which had previously been called The Osborne. Mr Sutcliffe had taken over the hotel in 1951 moving from the Empress Hotel in the Square (now the Nat West Bank).

The Empress Hotel in the Square, 1903

Empress Hotel, 1969
This area became the roundabout leading into the BIC.

Southlea in Durley Road was demolished in November 1982 as part of the transport policy for an access road to the BIC. To ease traffic from the A338 the route was changed to Durley Chine Road. Southlea was originally built as a summer residence for a bishop. After having been there for eighteen years, its last owners Mr and Mrs Ross moved to St George Hotel, West Cliff Gardens.

Southlea, 1981

The forward move by Bournemouth in diversifying its tourism was remarked upon by Mr Montague of English Tourism: "It is the responsibility of the town to keep up to date and I congratulate Bournemouth on doing this." However, it did not stop the cancellation of Ice Follies, for the first time apart from the war years, due to the recession and spiralling costs. Tourism had been hit by the recession but it had not contracted as much as manufacturing in Britain. In January 1991 the ice rink closed saying the lack of parking and competition from the ice rink at Poole's Tower Park led to its demise.

In August 1981 the shopping centre the Dalkeith Arcade was unveiled. The façade of the Dalkeith Hotel had been kept. It was originally the home of local riding master Henry Laidlow (from Dalkeith in Scotland) who had bought the land from the Dean Estate in 1871. In 1881 Mr Laidlow established a horse drawn omnibus service in Bournemouth, calling it 'Tally Ho'. By 1901 the building was the Dalkeith Private and Residential Hotel, the proprietor C Bartsch advertising "every home comfort studied". By 1906 it was Hotel Dalkeith with "dainty French and English cuisine". EL Jones assured: "No charge for baths, lights or attendance."

Dalkeith Hotel, 1927

Which put in its report (October 1981) that Bournemouth was "rather classy and landscaped whilst catering for older people, more recently livened up making it more popular with young people too".

A survey commissioned by the Council into its tourism policy was lambasted as providing no answers. Its aim had been to identify weaknesses in organisation and provision of tourism facilities and to suggest improvements. The Tourism Policy and Publicity Committee spoke of financial restraints and were accused of paying lip service to the hoteliers.

The piecemeal attitude to planning was criticised by the local Hotel Association. They argued it wasn't enough just to build new shops; they needed visitors to be spending in them. The town needed a balance between shops, wet weather facilities and entertainment venues. The Pavilion ballroom was losing money and without tourism the town would just be another backwater with a beach.

In 1988 it was thought that Bournemouth had between 10,000 and 12,000 bedrooms in around 1,200 hotels and guesthouses with around half having en-suite bathrooms. Visitor numbers remained fairly static with about two million staying 10 million bed nights with 10% being foreign students. Some hoteliers were however finding trading difficult and sold out to property developers as Bournemouth clamped down on nursing home conversions. Five hotels by Boscombe pier ceased trading and were replaced by flats.

Boscombe Beach, 1900s
The hotels in the background were demolished and replaced by flats.

Boscombe was viewed as needing serious help due its reputation as a drug centre and its general unkempt appearance. A plan was put forward for the Overstrand and Pier in July 1989 for a Water World Park with white water rides and a jungle theme.

The poor economy and rise in mortgage rates affected the summer trade with more day-trippers and hotels reporting people staying for a shorter time. The earlier anticipation of a 20% rise in domestic tourism had not materialised. Bournemouth was mocked by Blackpool's tourism chief: "Bournemouth is like Torquay and that market has gone. People don't want grass and trees, what they want is a good time. Sixteen million can't be wrong."

The Council however were not keen to see hotel stock go as they thought it would weaken the BIC's competitiveness against other conference centres as hotel prices would rise. To stem the flow the Council decided to designate the East Cliff as a Conservation area and the tourism committee would vet all applications for change of use involving hotels.

Other hotels had taken in visiting unemployed people, which was viewed as making the area detrimental to other holidaymakers. This obviously affected the tourist trade, with the accommodation capacity of the town quoted as being 55,000 in 1986 with only 1 in 20 visitors being from overseas. The problem arose again in 1993 with the recession-hit hotels as property agents let out hotels to those on housing benefit. Other hoteliers feared parts of

Boscombe, Westbourne and the East Cliff were being dragged down-market.

The Council wanted to attract a new hotel with meeting rooms and at least 200 bedrooms but few hotel groups showed any interest. Local hoteliers were horrified, as they believed existing accommodation should be upgraded along with tourist facilities and more emphasis placed on marketing. 1987 had been a poor trading year for tourists and they had cut prices in August to try and tempt holidaymakers. A survey had revealed Bournemouth was viewed as having nice walks, gardens and entertainment but it was too hilly and the sparse car parking expensive. It was pointed out that the town was getting left behind rival resorts such as Blackpool and needed to spend money on promotion and improvements to the town. Hard-pressed hoteliers grumbled that they were always the ones who paid the costs of attracting visitors when everyone profited from the business.

Norfolk Royale, 1969

Three major hotels hoping to benefit from the conference trade and business generated by finance companies moving it to the town undertook major refurbishing. The Norfolk Royale had been bought from FJB hotels in 1986 for £1¼ million and was spending £5 million, an overspend of £2¼ million due to structural problems on a 48-bedroom extension, 80-seat restaurant, underground parking for 88 cars, leisure and conference facilities.

The ground floor was reinforced, the three boilers replaced and the hotel rewired and re-plumbed. Room occupancy was expected to reach 60% with 35%-40% coming from conference trade, 15% from local business and 12% from weekend breaks. A double/twin room cost £100, a single room £75 and a suite £145.

The Royal Bath was also refurbished at a cost of £2½ million with a new indoor leisure centre and an overhaul of the public areas, stepping up its investment after the sale of neighbouring Marsham Court Hotel for £2 million.

The Oak Bar, Marsham Court, 1960s

The occupancy level for the Royal Bath Hotel in 1987 had been 60% with an average room rate of £60. The hotel was often the first choice for headquarters for conferences at the BIC.

The Carlton was spending £1¼ milion on a new reception, library and kitchen. They did not see themselves as competing with other hotels in town but with Chewton Glen in New Milton. The new owner of the Carlton, Mr Losel, wanted to return the hotel to being the only privately owned 5-star hotel in Britain. Staff numbers were cut by half; some timeshares bought back and a leisure centre planned in the basement. The hotel charged £75 for a single, £95 for twin/double and £225-£250 for a timeshare. They expected to raise prices once the bedrooms had been refurbished.

Smaller hotels were also upgrading. Maureen and Manfred Heller's Belvedere had been upgraded to a 3-star and they had bought the neighbouring Hotel Cecil with plans to link the two properties. Room occupancy was around 70% with half being business customers paying £24 B&B. (*Caterer and Hotel Keeper* January 1988)

Belvedere Hotel, 1980s

The 1990s saw a transformation in the town; upgrading of the polytechnic to university status brought in thousands of youngsters adding to the large number of foreign students. The town began to lose its 'God's waiting room' image and attractions such as the controversial Waterfront building, pub chains opening premises along Old Christchurch Road, numerous nightclubs and the remodelling of The Square ensured the town was still alive and kicking!

However in the early nineties the recession was still being felt although Bournemouth was voted Top Resort in England in 1992 due to its: "clean, fresh, cared for appearance and the absence of derelict buildings." Tourism was also the biggest employer in town; twelve thousand people were seen as a conservative estimate of employees as it spilled over into shops, restaurants, taxis, entertainment etc. bringing £300 million into the local economy.

In 1992 Richard Carr and his Allied Leisure group pulled out of a £15 million scheme for Bournemouth Pier and a marina at Boscombe as the shares slumped from 108.5p to 18p. Other operators wanted to have a Sealife Centre and shops on the pier.

In July 1993 a £100 million Sea Gardens scheme was put forward to revamp the seafront. The Art College would move to Honeycombe Chine. Boscombe Pier would be renovated and a monorail was to run between the piers. Tented international trade pavilions would be on the Undercliff. Plans were also submitted for rejuvenating Bournemouth Pier including the formation of an ocean liner shape.

Trade was still suffering from the recession, cheap holidays abroad, the IRA bombing of a Brighton hotel in August 1993 and the vagaries of the

146

weather. Hotels were shutting down unable to undergo the investment many of them needed. For the smaller hotel/guesthouse putting in 'en-suites' was expensive and it often reduced the number of rooms available. Refurbishment had to be done though as visitors used to continental hotels wanted the same facilities in hotels back home. Larger hotels faced bankruptcy putting in indoor swimming pools. *The Times* had run an article in July 1992 describing Bournemouth as "shivering in cold winds of recession". The numbers of visitors were down and three large hotels were in the hands of the receiver. In fact by January 1993 the largest hotel owner in Bournemouth was the Official Receiver although the hotels were open and being run as normal.

"Bournemouth is in danger of dying a slow death" business leaders warned as another project, the Sea Gardens was rejected by planners. The town lacked an image, had outmoded hotel rooms and declining shopping facilities. The advertising campaign using slogans such as "Bourne without Equal" had not worked. The town was seen as lacking a corporate policy and image and needed more coordinate marketing. A survey revealed people thought Bournemouth too expensive and there was nothing for young people to do. It was argued nightclubs should be allowed to stay open later as happened in rival resorts.

Booking patterns changed as visitors left it to the last minute to see if they could in fact afford a holiday. Dinners in hotels were down as guests opted to go out instead for a cheaper meal. Luis Candal from the Bournemouth International Centre advised that hotels should reassess their pricing policies.

The conference trade did bring in a new type of customer to help the shoulder months (those months either side of 'high season') as August was no longer a month to be relied on for the hotels to be full. The summer of 1993 saw 60% of hotels business stagnated with the smaller guesthouses being squeezed out by larger hotels offering special rates. Stays were becoming shorter and the Saturday-to-Saturday bookings almost non-existent, passing trade was on the decline and more visitors were making last minute bookings. This was even more apparent a few years later with the Internet when people looked up hotel websites and booked just hours before coming to Bournemouth, especially if the weather was good.

By 1994 tourism bookings were in a dire state. There had been bad national publicity with the DHSS hostels, prostitutes and nightmare traffic reports. There was a lack of funds and summer visitors mingled with armed police. In October the Government failed to recognise the importance of tourism and cut funding to the English Tourist Board. It was seen as ironic by the trade that the IRA had chosen English resorts as a target to bomb as they saw them as being an important part of England's tourism industry.

From May 1995 some hotels including the Carlton, Swallow Highcliff and Langtry Manor took advantage of the new law allowing weddings on their premises. By November 1995 a new attraction, the Imax, with a sixty-foot screen was announced as an answer to the hotels call for wet weather attractions.

Hotels were still seeing room occupancy declining. The local Hotel Association wanted a debate within the Town Council using its planning powers to determine the economic level of tourism beds necessary to support Bournemouth tourism's infrastructure. The hotels were concerned with the discounting they needed to do to attract visitors, due to what they saw as over capacity in the town. The English Tourist Board believed Bournemouth had 25,000 bed spaces, 300 hotels, 12,000 hotel rooms, 200 guesthouses and 200 offering self-catering.

The Council were embracing the World Wide Web with visitors being able to book via the Internet. It would "bring Bournemouth to the attention of the world". By February 1998 *Harpers and Queen* declared the town "next coolest city on the planet". It was however a very unseasonably hot February and a guest from the Durley Grange Hotel had to be treated for sunstroke and not a heart attack as first thought!

Many of the town's biggest hotels such as Connaught, Norfolk Royale and Queens announced that they would not be opening for the Millennium New Year celebrations as staff and entertainment costs were too high.

The New Era

Despite being voted "Resort of the Year 2000" by *Holiday Which* some hotels were struggling. Plans to demolish the Savoy and to rebuild it as a 65-bed hotel and 8-storey high block of flats were refused as it was deemed to be a landmark building. In 1920 it was advertised as being "High Class throughout" and the most "beautifully situated, furnished and constructed hotel in Bournemouth". (*Mates, Beautiful Bournemouth*) The New Savoy Hotel as managed by Mr and Mrs Odlum was one of England's best. Harry Brown formerly of Marsham Court and Melford Hall also managed it when in 1950 the hotel was advertised as having: "Best features of the luxury Continental Hotels with English comfort." It is now mainly trading as a coaching hotel.

Savoy Hotel, 1960s

St Georges Hotel in West Cliff Gardens and the Winter Gardens Hotel were also refused permission to be demolished. Meanwhile in June 2001, The East Cliff Court had a serious fire after its refurbishment with 20 guest and 20 staff led to safety. It wasn't to reopen until the following year.

The redevelopment of the Winter Gardens saga rumbled on with Richard Carr's scheme being turned down in favour of a new hotel and flats which were seen as more acceptable. New schemes, which had opened such as The

Waterfront complex, were not well received as the Imax cinema failed to open on time. The Obscura Café was also seen as ugly, the food expensive and the Obscura Camera was rarely available to view. The Russell Cotes Museum and Art Gallery and the railway station however successfully completed their major refurbishments.

The Foot and Mouth epidemic in 2001 did not have such a serious impact in Bournemouth as some other places had but it was another reason for visitors to choose holidays abroad. Hoteliers were furious with Tourism Minister Kim Howells in July 2001 for his sweeping statement on English hotels: "Hotels ripping off guests, paying slave wages and characterless shabby bland décor." The beleaguered hoteliers felt that support would have been more appropriate especially with all the extra regulations, climate charge levy and only £3½ million foot and mouth emergency funding being granted to England compared to the £13½ million that Scotland received.

Slavanka Hotel in Southbourne, 2006
Now demolished and replaced with a residential care home

The local Hotel Association were calling for change of use for hotels and guesthouses to be governed by market forces as they saw the town as being overstocked with bed spaces. The head of tourism Ken Male defended the

Council's position. "One of the reasons Bournemouth has succeeded over the years is because it has such a wide range of beds available within walking distance of the BIC. If this is not maintained the provision of facilities will be jeopardised. It also poses a major threat to areas like Southbourne where more and more hotels are being converted to flats."

Plans were announced in 2001 for a new cinema complex, restaurants and bars on the old bus station site. The out-dated cinemas would move from what was becoming a fairly run down Westover Road. However it appears to have gone the way of other schemes in the town, which emerge, plans passed and then forgotten about.

Despite the BIC being voted Top Conference Venue in 1995 and reopening after a refurbishment in 2005, new conference centres in other towns including the urban cities of Manchester and Liverpool make inroads into Bournemouth's slice of the conference trade. In June 2007 tourism was said to have brought £400 million to the local economy with business tourism bringing in £137 million through the hotels and the BIC. The Political Party conferences despite bringing security problems raise the profile of the town. Conference trade is anticipated to be down in 2009 due to the recession.

The Travelodge
Christchurch Road, Boscombe

The Ramada Encore

Hotels in Bournemouth continued struggling with low occupancy levels and some closed down. The Avon Royal and Hazelwood Hotels on Christchurch Road after years of wrangling were demolished and a 107 bed Travelodge opened in May 2005. The budget hotels had arrived.

The Pavilion Hotel on Bath Road was pulled down and a much larger, modern design Ramada Encore built in its place, opening in 2006. It was said that in that year Bournemouth had 14,000 bed spaces with an average occupancy being 60%. However, although the number of hotels had decreased the remaining hotels did not see an increase in occupancy. The local Hotel Association was worried that large chain hotels would not commit to Bournemouth's marketing budget as they used their own national campaigns.

The Cadogan and East Anglia Hotels on Poole Road were demolished to make way for a Premier Inn in 2008. In 2006 the old Palace Court which had been a Hilton, then Metro was sold and was expected to be a 4-star Golden Tulip hotel. However, it became the town's third Premier Inn in 2008. The other Premier Inn being Lynton Court which had not been run as a hotel for about twenty years. The Tralee Hotel on the West Cliff is currently being redeveloped as another Travelodge. It will nearly double its bedroom capacity from 59 to 110.

Premier Inn, Poole Road, Bournemouth

Bournemouth is changing and the days of hotels being independently owned and the Bournemouth 'hotel families' will soon be gone. It has been said that in other towns powerful hotel chains use their marketing muscle and independent hotels find it hard to compete and close down. This started in Bournemouth with chain stores and cafés and now there are corporate chain hotels.

However Bournemouth has proved itself to be resilient and able to adapt itself to changing times. Despite the current recession many hotels are refurbishing and looking forward to the town attracting more visitors. The Air Festival has put Bournemouth at the forefront of sensational free events. The surf reef is known all over the world and the new dance centre will hopefully add another dimension to the town's superb entertainment package.

The Cumberland Hotel
Refurbished in 2006, still reflecting its original Art Deco grandeur

In 2010 Bournemouth celebrates its bi-centenary and can look proudly at what it has achieved and the hotels can view their own important place in shaping the town. It certainly would be a very different place without the hotels both small and large. I wish them all success for the future.

Bibliography and Sources

A Century of Service	J. Wilson
A History of the Bourne Tregonwell Estate	A.J. Miller
Auction Sale, Valuable & Freehold Interest 1921	
Beautiful Bournemouth 1920	
Bournemouth & The First World War	M.A. Edgington
Bournemouth & The Second World	M.A. Edgington
Bournemouth Bulletin	Bournemouth Hotel Association
Bournemouth Echo	
Bournemouth Guides	
Bournemouth Highcliff	N. Redman (Whitbread Archivist)
Bournemouth Illustrated 1896	
Bournemouth The Good Old Days	Rodney Legg
Bright's Illustrated Guide to Bournemouth 1888	
Burgess Rolls	
Caterer & Hotelkeeper June 1973	
Hancock	Freddie Hancock & David Natha
Heywoods Guide to Bournemouth 1886	
Mates An Illustrated Account of Bournemouth 1893	
Mates Hampshire & Isle of Wight Illustrated 1899	
Secrets, Boyhood in a Jewish Hotel 1932-54	Ronald Hayman
The Book of Bournemouth	David & Rita Popham
The Book of Bournemouth	Dr Watson Smith
The Evolution & Transformation of Fashionable Resort Regions	J.W.N. Soarce
The Royal Bath	Peter Pugh
The Times	
Thousand Shall Fall	M. Peden
Viewpoint	Bournemouth Hotel Association